Basic Developing & Printing in Black and White

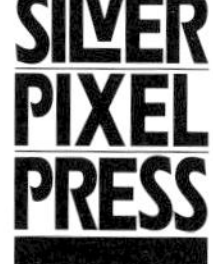

Basic Developing & Printing in Black and White

There are many good reasons for knowing something about making pictures as well as just taking them. You may need to know how to develop film and make prints to earn a merit badge, complete a 4-H project, or make illustrations for a science fair. Maybe you're taking or teaching a photography course in school or at camp.

Perhaps you need to learn something about these techniques to make pictures for your business. Or maybe you picked up this book for the most enjoyable reason of all: because making your own black-and-white enlargements sounds like fun. Readers may notice that this book is done entirely in black and white. We have chosen to do so to celebrate and emphasize this unique medium. Whatever your reason for wanting to know about developing, printing, and enlarging, we think you'll find this book a fine introduction for beginners of all ages.

Professional film-processing services (photofinishers) do excellent work and unless you're really bitten by the home-darkroom bug, you might want to let them make most of your pictures. But by doing your own work, you gain more control over the results. You can make prints lighter or darker to suit your needs, enlarge from a small area of a negative, and make prints for any size you want. The cost is modest, and it's a lot of fun.

Before you start a project like this, it's a good idea to know where you're going. So here's a brief outline of how we plan to do things.

First you'll learn to process your black-and-white film. Of course, if you already have some acceptable black-and-white negatives you can start making prints right away. This is a good idea because you'll also have prints made by a photofinisher to compare with your results.

Making a proof sheet of your negatives comes next, followed by making an enlargement from a negative. You'll also learn different techniques to help improve your enlargements.

Finally, you'll learn how to set up a darkroom and how to do some fun things with your hobby. There's also a chapter with tips on choosing a photographic paper and a list of different chemicals you can use to process and print your films. All these things are explained, step by step, in the pages that follow.

The Kodak materials described in this publication are available from dealers who normally supply Kodak products. Other materials may be used, but equivalent results may not be obtained.

For Your Safety

Care is required in handling all chemicals. Photochemicals are no exception. For example, we recommend that you wear protective gloves to prevent skin contact with many photographic chemicals. You can normally obtain safe handling information for a particular Kodak chemical from the product label or the Material Safety Data Sheet (available from Communications and Public Affairs Publications, 343 State Street, Rochester, New York 14650, or in the U.S., call the toll-free number 1-800-242-2424).

Processing Film

When you take a picture, light reflected from the scene strikes the film and makes a latent image. This image is invisible. Now we need something that will convert the latent image into one we can see and use. That's the job of developer.

After development, all the light parts of the scene are dark and all the dark parts are light, giving a negative version of the original scene.

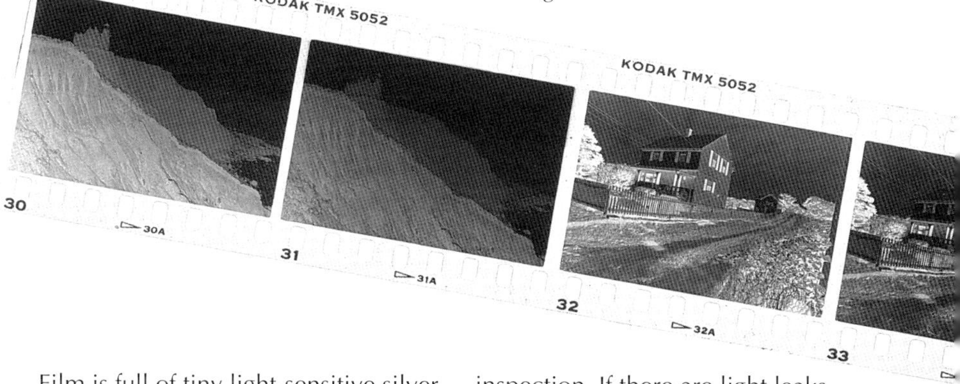

Film is full of tiny light-sensitive silver halide particles. The particles that have been struck by light turn black when they're put into the developer. After development, all the light parts of the scene are dark and all the dark parts are light, giving a negative version of the original scene.

You'll need a darkroom only briefly for processing film. Any room that you can completely darken will do. You can use a closet, the basement, or your kitchen. If you want to set up a permanent darkroom, see the chapter starting on page 48.

You must load the film into the processing tank in complete darkness. All the other steps can be carried out in regular room light. Here's a good test to make sure your room is dark enough. Sit in the room you're going to use as a darkroom for 5 minutes with the lights turned off. After 5 minutes, if you can't see a sheet of white paper placed against a dark background, the room passes inspection. If there are light leaks, cover them with heavy cloth or opaque tape. Use a rug to cover the crack under the door.

Mix all your chemicals with water at the temperature given in the chemical instructions. Rinse the measuring cup between uses so that you don't contaminate one solution with another. Process one roll, and look at your results before doing any more.

The result of this darkroom effort should be a usable negative, if you exposed the film correctly. You'll soon learn the appearance of a properly exposed and properly developed negative. It will have considerable detail, even in the lightest and darkest portions. It's not all dark or all light. The illustrations of negatives on pages 14, 15, 36 and 37 show what to look for.

Try to evaluate your own negatives. A very common fault is overdevelopment, which produces dark, dense negatives.

When you take a picture, light reflected from the scene strikes the film and makes a latent image. This image is invisible. It is made visible by processing in special chemicals.

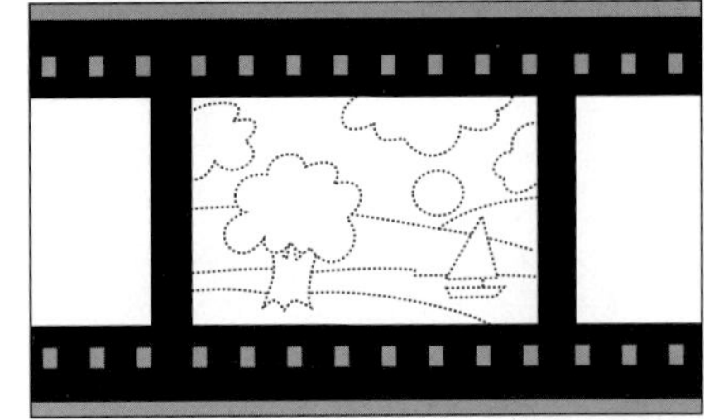

Film is full of tiny light-sensitive silver halide particles. The particles that have been struck by light turn black when they are processed in the first chemical—the developer.

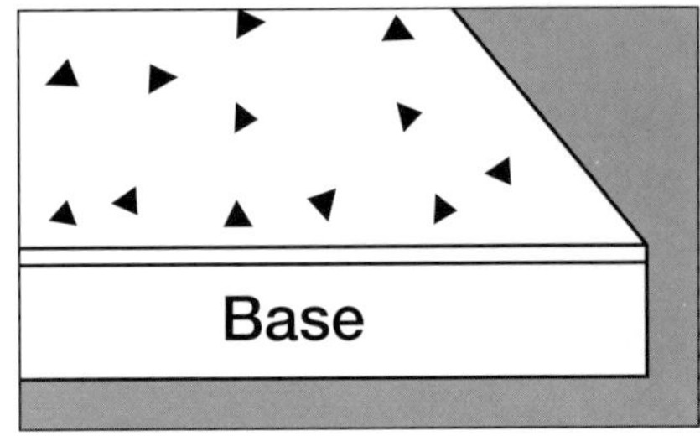

The particles that have not been struck by light will not change in the developer.

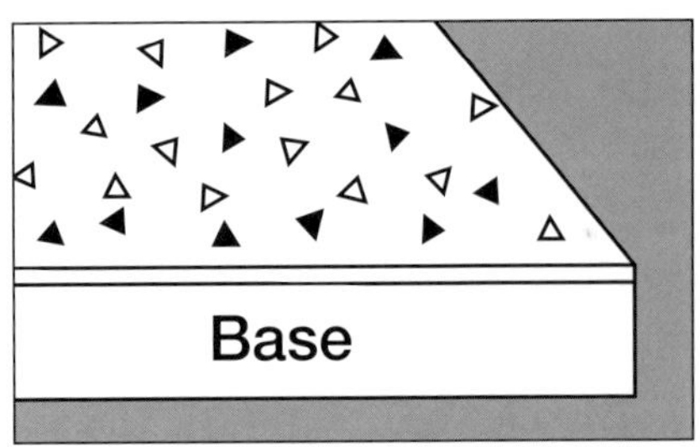

The unexposed silver grains are later made soluble by a processing step called fixing and are washed out of the film.

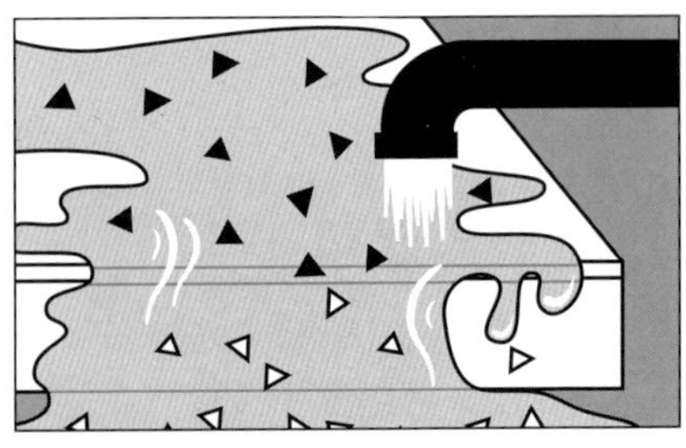

The remaining particles of black metallic silver have formed a visible image, called a negative, in which the original tones are reversed. The light parts of the scene are dark, and the dark parts are light.

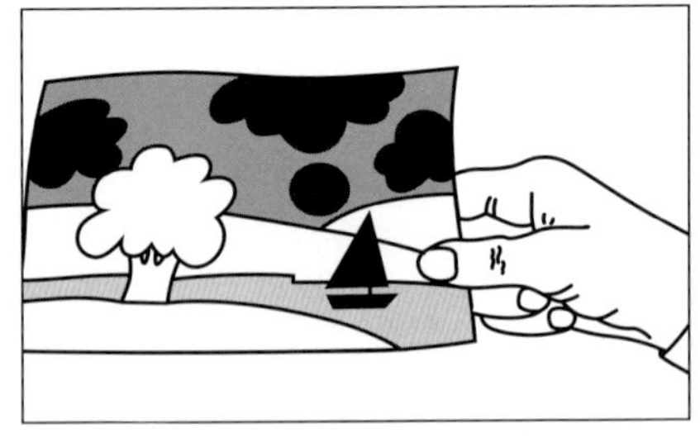

The scientific way to avoid over- and underdevelopment is to use the time-temperature approach. Develop for the recommended time at the recommended temperature, and you can hardly help but get good negatives. These recommendations are listed below and some are included in the instructions for most Kodak black-and-white films.

The recommended temperature for most black-and-white film developers is 68°F (20°C). For KODAK T-MAX Developer, the recommendation is 75°F (24°C). Maybe you can't adjust your solutions to that temperature for some reason. When your solutions are warmer, you have to develop for less than the usual time, because chemical reactions are fastest at higher temperatures. By the same token, if solutions are colder you must use longer-than-normal developing time. Exactly how long? Check the table below. **Primary recommendations are in bold type.**

Developing Times (in minutes)—Small Tank*

KODAK Film and Developer	65°F (18°C)	68°F (20°C)	70°F (21°C)	72°F (22°C)	75°F (24°C)
VERICHROME Pan					
D-76	8	**7**	5 ½	5	4 ½
D-76 (1:1)	11	**9**	8	7	6
HC-110 (1:31)	6	**5**	4 ½	4	2
MICRODOL-X	10	**9**	8	7	6
PLUS-X Pan					
T-MAX	6 ½	5 ½	5 ½	5	**5**
D-76	6 ½	**5 ½**	5	4 ½	3 3/4
D-76 (1:1)	8	**7**	6 ½	6	5
HC-110 (1:31)	6	**5**	4 ½	4	3 ½
MICRODOL-X	8	**7**	6 ½	6	5 ½
TRI-X Pan					
T-MAX	7	6	6	5 ½	**5 ½**
D-76	9	**8**	7 ½	6 ½	5 ½
D-76 (1:1)	11	**10**	9 ½	9	8
HC-110 (1:31)	8 ½	**7 ½**	6 ½	6	5
MICRODOL-X	11	**10**	9 ½	9	8
T-MAX 100 Professional					
T-MAX	NR	8	7 ½	7	**6 ½**
D-76	10 ½	**9**	8	7	6
D-76 (1:1)	14 ½	**12**	11	10	8 ½
HC-110 (1:31)	8	**7**	6 ½	6	5
MICRODOL-X	16	**13 ½**	12	10 ½	8 ½
T-MAX 400 Professional					
T-MAX	NR	7	6 ½	6 ½	**6**
D-76	9	**8**	7	6 ½	5 ½
D-76 (1:1)	14 ½	**12 ½**	11	10	9
HC-110 (1:31)	6 ½	**6**	5 ½	5	4 ½
MICRODOL-X	12	**10 ½**	9	8 ½	7 ½

* Agitation at 30-second intervals throughout development
NR=Not recommended

Things You'll Need

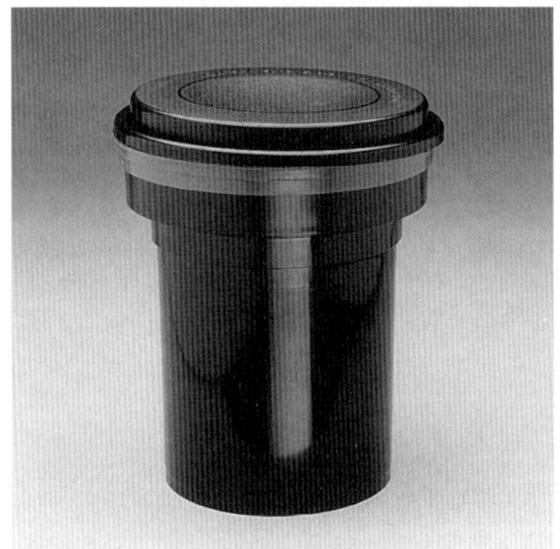

1 A light-tight processing tank, such as a Paterson Tank, with a reel designed to accept your film size.

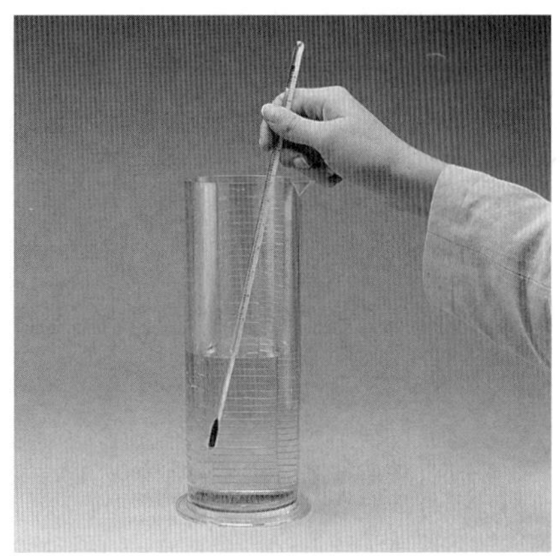

2 A darkroom thermometer to measure temperatures of solutions.

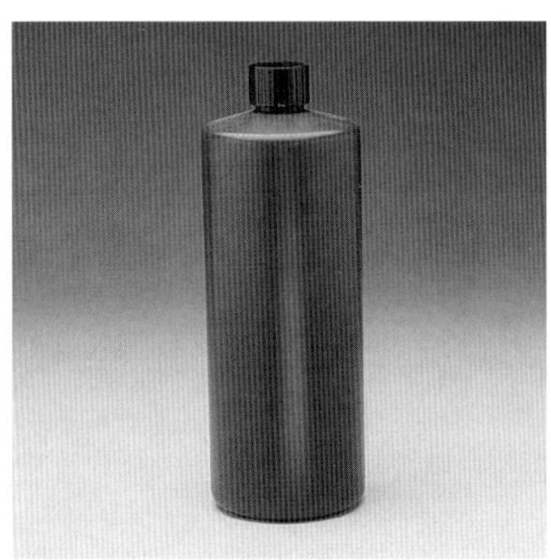

5 Three large bottles like the one shown above.

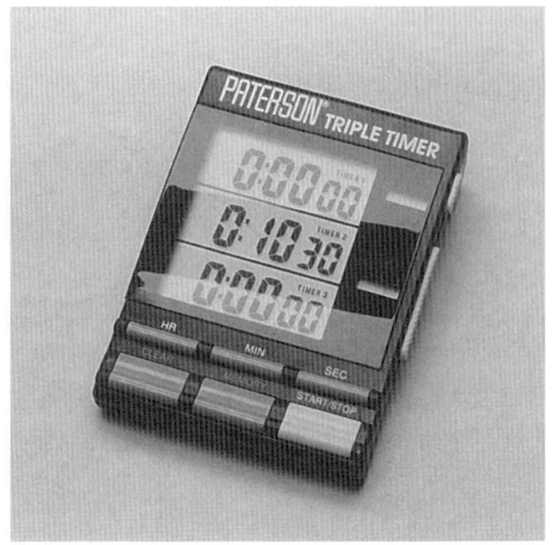

6 A darkroom timer or a clock with a sweep-second hand.

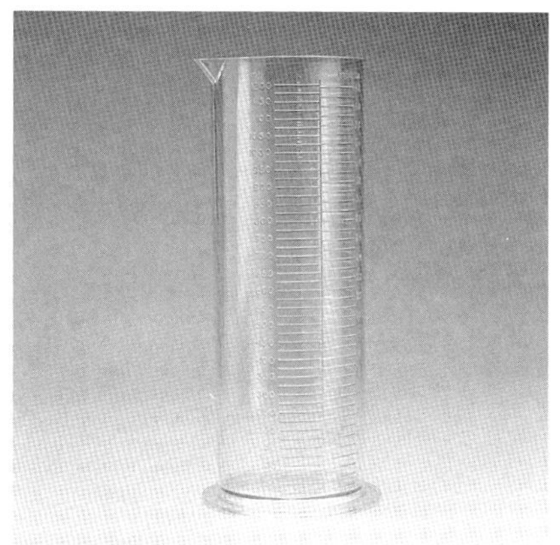

3 *A 42-ounce (1200 ml) darkroom graduate or kitchen measuring cup.*

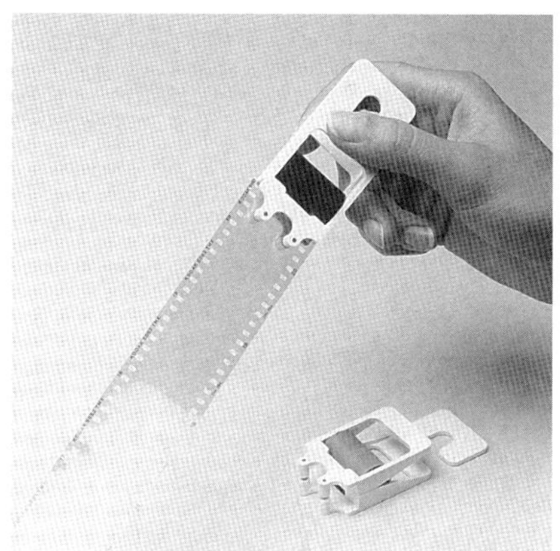

4 *Film clips or spring-type clothespins.*

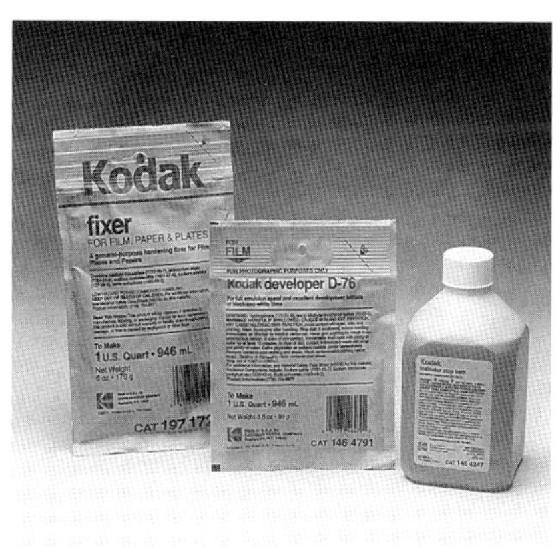

7 *Chemicals: KODAK Fixer, Developer, and Stop Bath.*

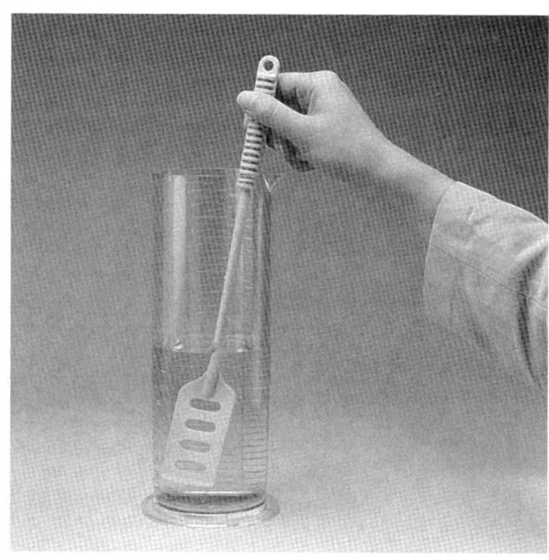

8 *A stirring rod to mix the chemicals.*

Film Developing

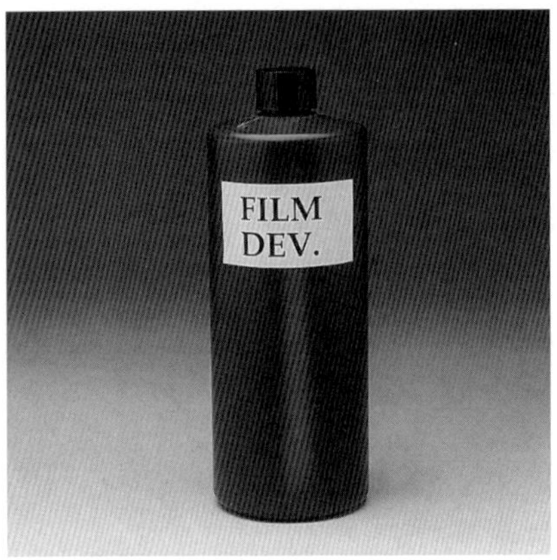

1 *In one of the bottles, mix the developer according to the package instructions. Label the bottle FILM DEVELOPER.*

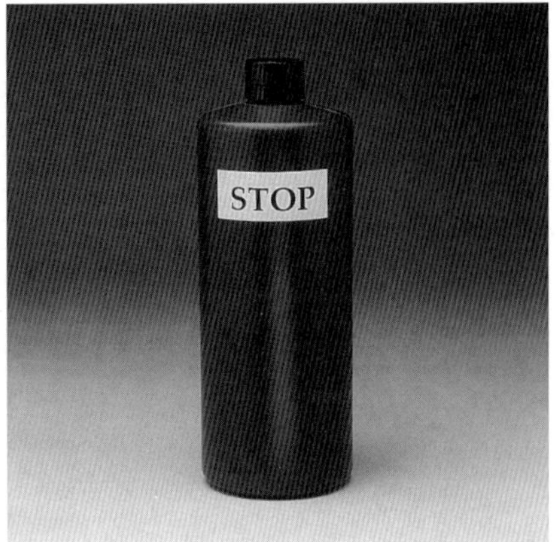

2 *In the second bottle, mix the stop bath according to the package instructions. Label the bottle STOP BATH or STOP.*

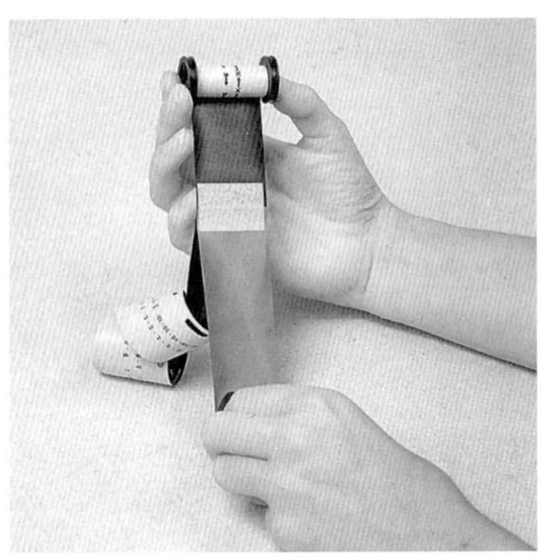

5 ***In total darkness,** prepare to load your film into the tank. If you're using roll film, rip off the EXPOSED sticker, and then separate the film and paper backing. The film is attached to the paper backing with a strip of tape. Detach the film and discard the paper and tape. Use a bottle-cap remover to open 35 mm magazines.*

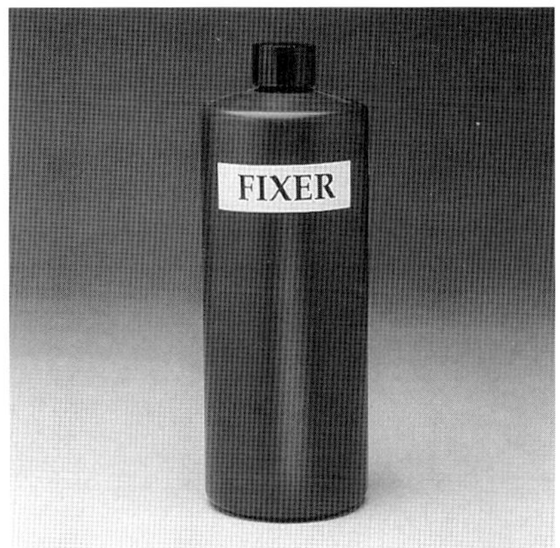

3 *In the third bottle, mix the fixer according to the package instructions. Label this bottle FIXER.*

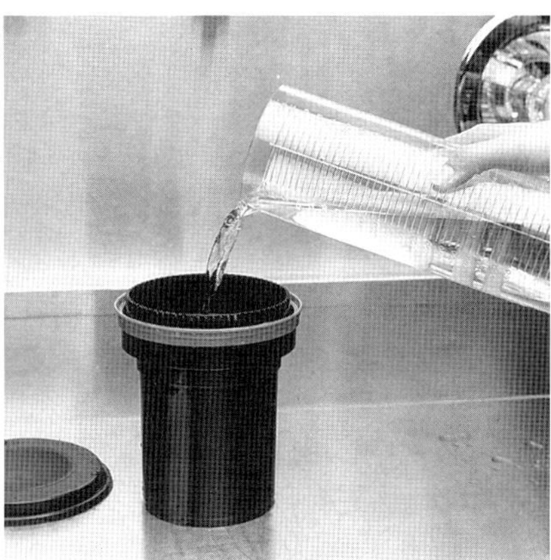

4 *Stabilize the developer at the temperature you selected from the table on page 7. (See tip below). Pour the required amount into the developing tank.*

TIP

Place your graduate (with developer) in a large, deep tray of warm or cool water until the temperature has stabilized. Instead of a tray, you could modify a 1-gallon (2-litre) plastic jug commonly used for household cleaning products, like bleach. Empty and thoroughly wash the jug. Cut the jug, in circumference, at the height of the solution in the graduate. Place the graduate in the jug with the warm or cool water until the desired temperature is reached. In either case, the water level should be at least equal to the level of solution in the graduate.

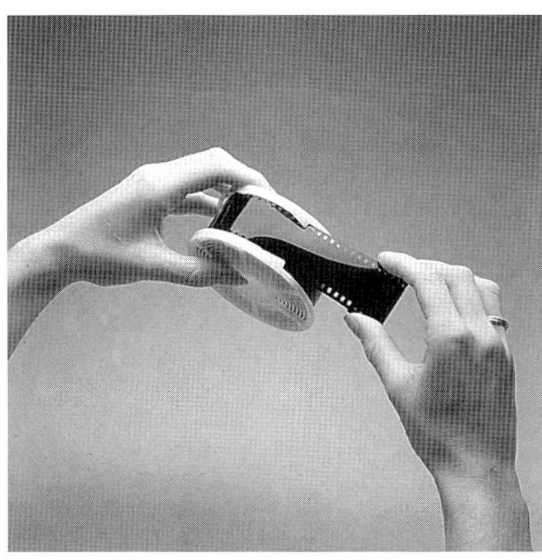

6 *Handling the film by the edges, roll it onto the reel according to the tank directions. Put the reel into the tank, secure the lid, and start timing. You may now turn on the room lights.*

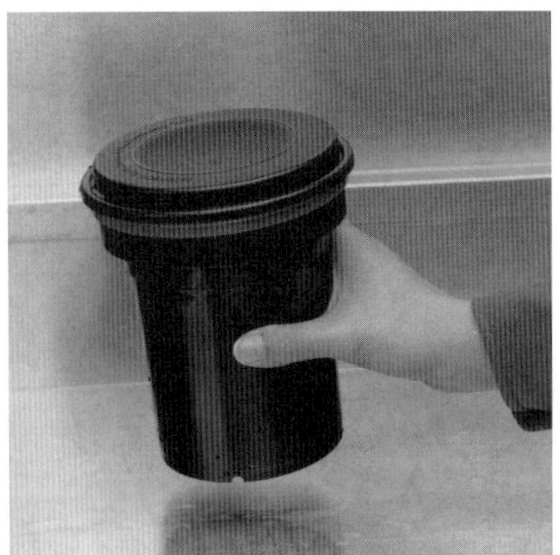

Tap the tank against your working surface to remove any air bubbles. After 30 seconds, agitate the tank by inverting it, rotating it in a circular motion, or rotating the reels. See the instructions for your tank. Do this for about 5 seconds at 30-second intervals. At the end of the recommended developing time, pour the solution back into the developer bottle. When pouring, tip the tank only slightly at the start.

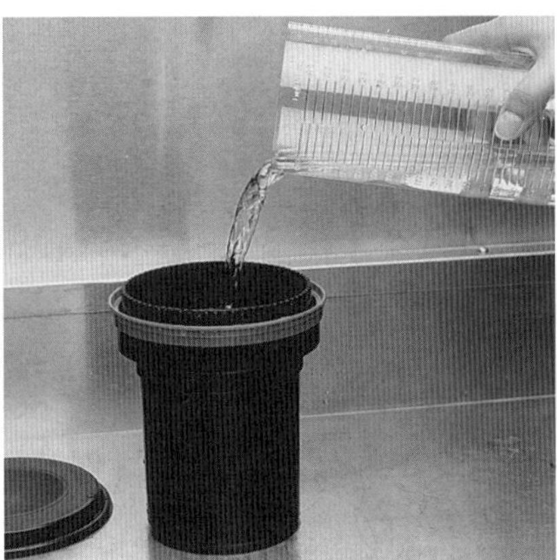

7 *Pour the stop-bath solution (stabilized at 65 to 75°F [18 to 24°C]) through the opening in the top. Do not open the tank. Agitate gently for about 30 seconds; then pour the liquid back into its original bottle.*

TIP

Rinse your graduate after each of the processing steps.

TIP

To shorten washing time (step 9), rinse the film in KODAK Hypo Clearing Agent (see page 65). First wash the film for 30 seconds. Next submerge it in a Hypo Clearing Agent solution for 1 to 2 minutes, with moderate agitation. Then wash for 5 minutes.

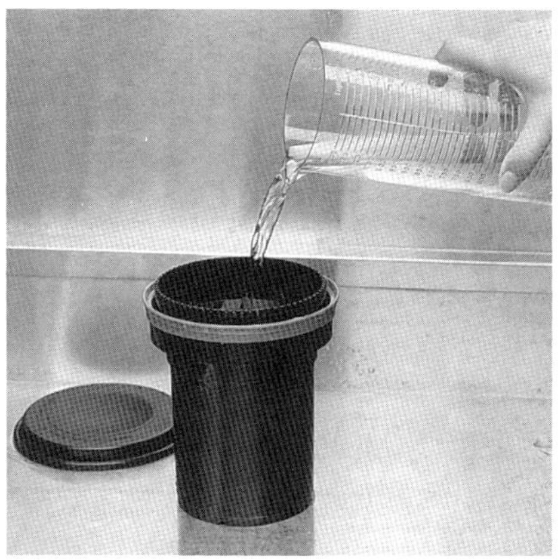

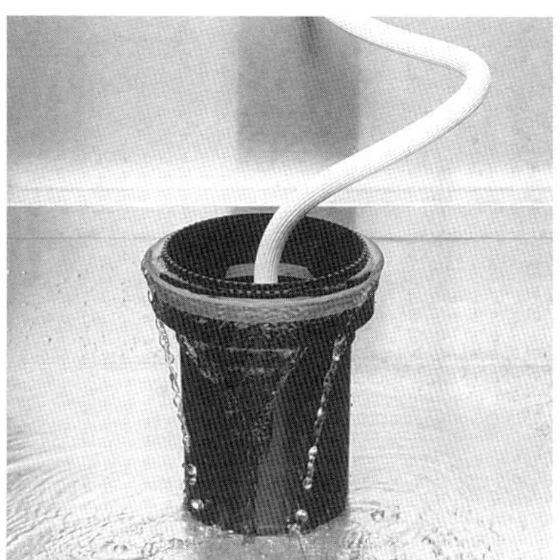

8 *Add the fixer solution (stabilized at 65 to 75°F [18 to 24°C]) and agitate for about 5 seconds at 30-second intervals. At the end of the fixing time (5 to 10 minutes), pour the solution into its bottle.*

9 *Remove the tank cover, place the tank under a moderate stream or hose of water at 65 to 75°F (18 to 24°C), and let the film wash for about a half hour.* *See tip on page 12.*

10 *Hang up the film with a film clip or clothespin at each end. Dampen a viscose sponge, wring it out, and then gently run it along both sides of the film to remove large droplets of water.*

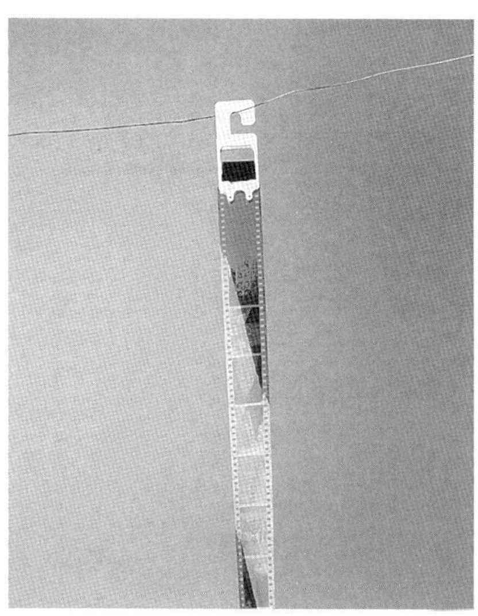

TIP

To eliminate the need for wiping the film and minimize water marks and drying streaks, rinse the film with diluted KODAK PHOTO-FLO Solution. Follow the instructions on the bottle, or use a film squeegee to remove any water. Let the film dry. Don't forget to rinse all parts of your film tank.

Troubleshooting

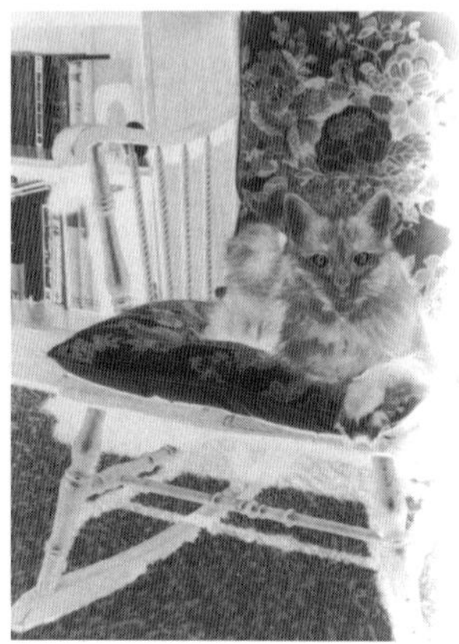

Streaky Negatives—Due to uneven development. Probably not all of the film was in contact with the developer throughout development time or there simply wasn't enough solution.

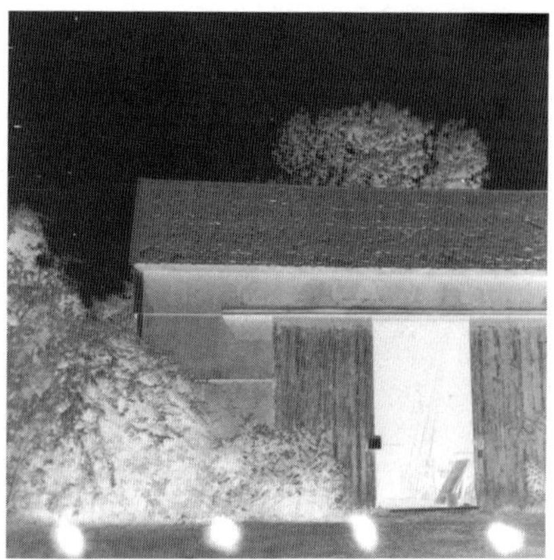

Rows of Regularly Spaced Marks—If they occur inside the picture area of the negative, it's because the film wasn't properly seated in the apron or reel or because you used the wrong apron.

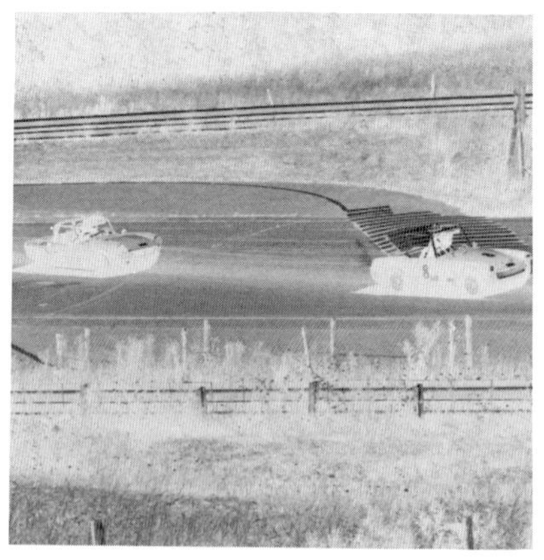

Thin, Very Transparent Negatives—If there are no really dark black areas in the entire negative, it usually means that your developer was too cold, the developing time was too short, or the negative was underexposed.

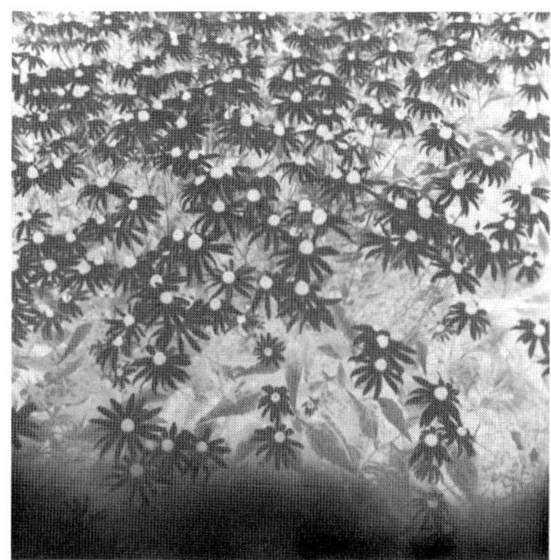

Black Streaks—A sign that light reached the film while you were loading or unloading your camera. If all the streaks are on the same side, it might be because the top of your developing tank was loosened during processing.

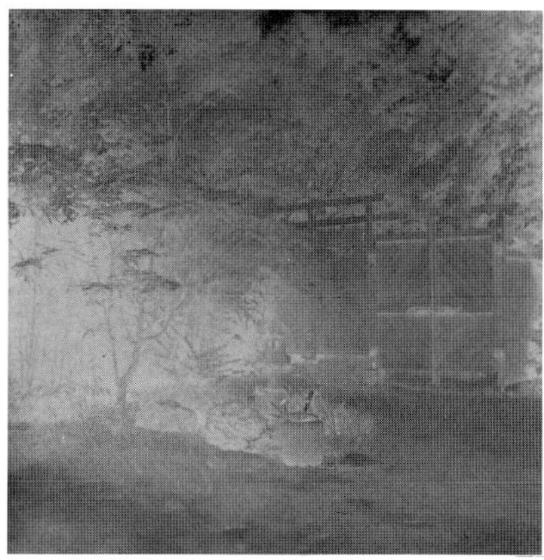

Overall Grayness—Often caused by light leaking into your darkroom during the time you were loading your developing tank.

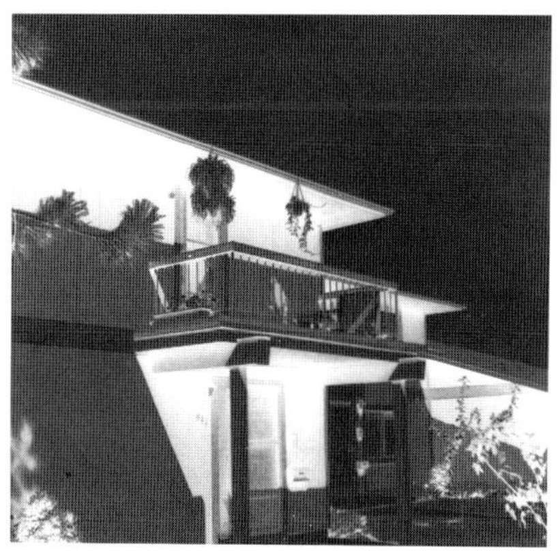

Dense, Heavy Negatives—This indicates that the developer was too warm, the film was developed too long, or the negative was overexposed.

Making Proof Sheets

Proof sheets consist of many prints made from a strip or strips of your negatives. These prints are the same size as your negatives. Proof sheets help you choose the best negatives for enlarging and make a good record to file with your negatives. Remember that your negatives won't all have the same density, so some of the individual prints on your proof sheet will be darker than others.

Proof sheets are made by placing negatives into contact with photographic paper. Light shining through the negative forms an image on the paper. When you immerse this paper into three successive solutions—developer, stop bath, and fixer—you end up with a proof sheet.

Since photographic paper is sensitive to light, you must handle it in a dark place. Paper isn't as sensitive to light as film, however, and you will be processing it under safelight illumination. For more information on darkrooms and safelight placement, see page 48.

Things You'll Need

1 *A printing frame and a 7-watt light bulb or an enlarger and a piece of window glass.*

You can make a printing frame by using a piece of window glass and a piece of composition board. Both pieces should be the same size. Put one piece on top of the other and use wide adhesive tape to make a hinge connecting the two pieces. (It's a good idea to tape the remaining edges of the glass so that you won't cut yourself.)

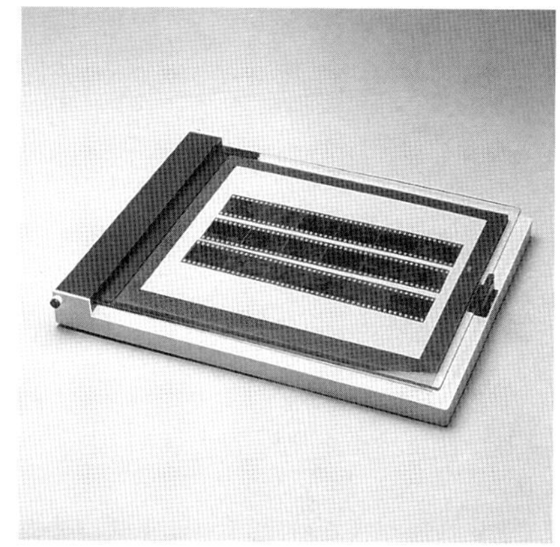

2 *Four trays such as Paterson Trays, 8 x 10 inches.*

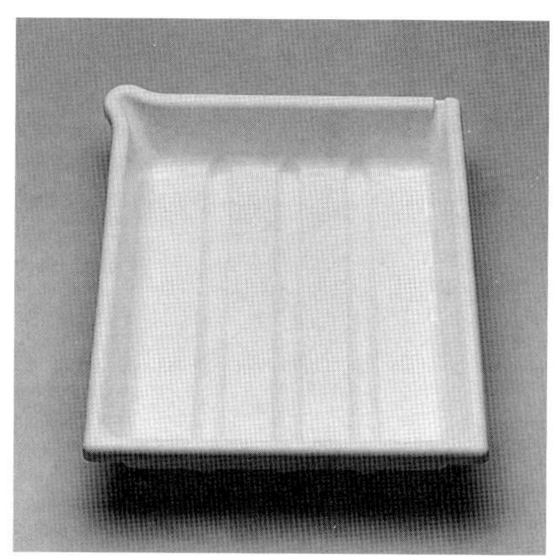

3 *A stirring rod to mix the chemicals.*

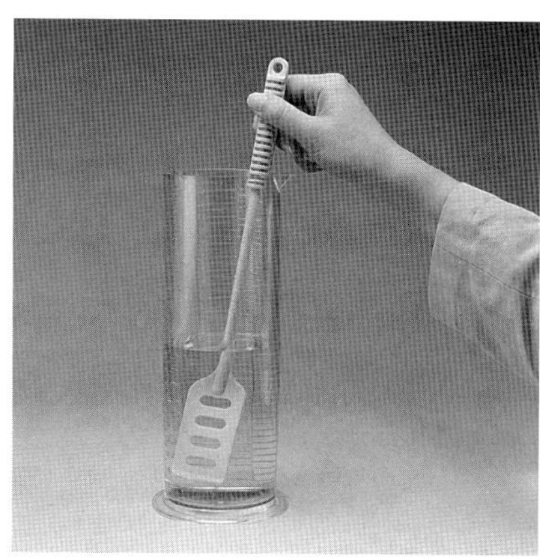

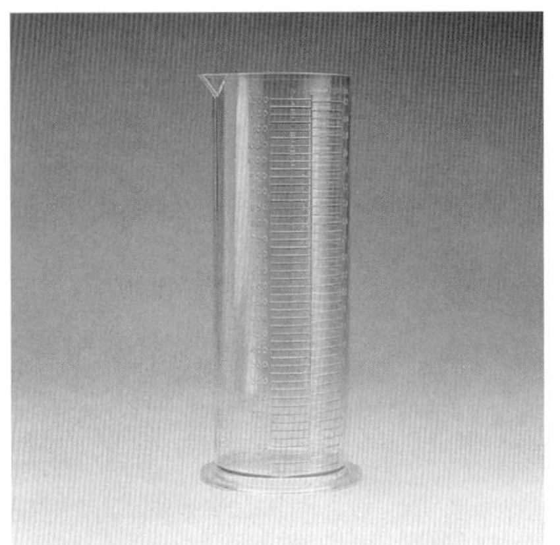

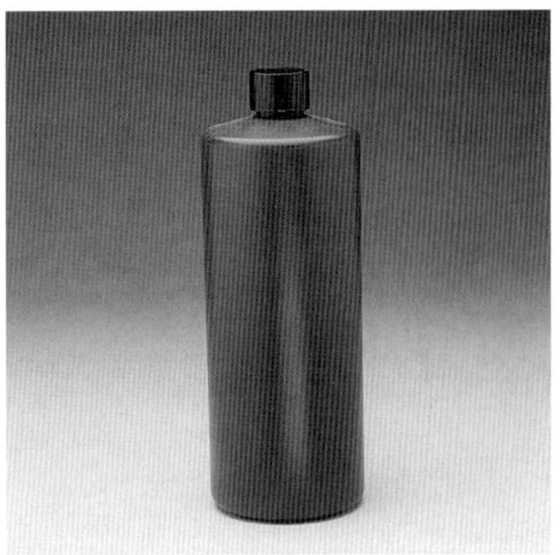

4 *A 42-ounce (1200 ml) darkroom graduate or kitchen measuring cup and 3 large bottles, such as the one shown above, to the right.*

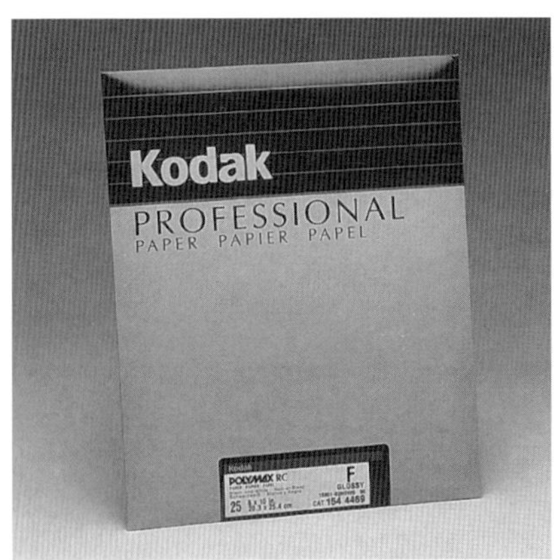

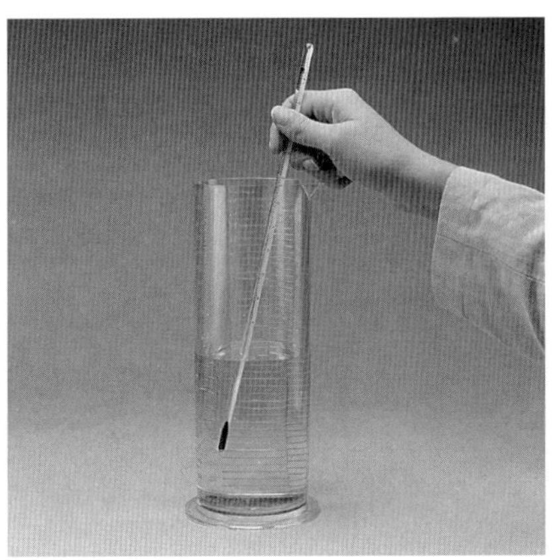

7 *Photographic paper such as KODAK POLYMAX RC Paper, 8 x 10 inches.*

8 *A darkroom thermometer to measure temperatures of solutions.*

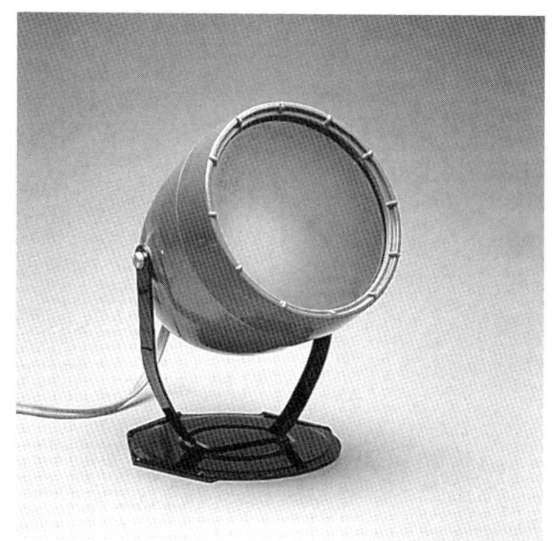

5 A safelight, such as a KODAK Darkroom Lamp with a KODAK OC Safelight Filter (light amber).

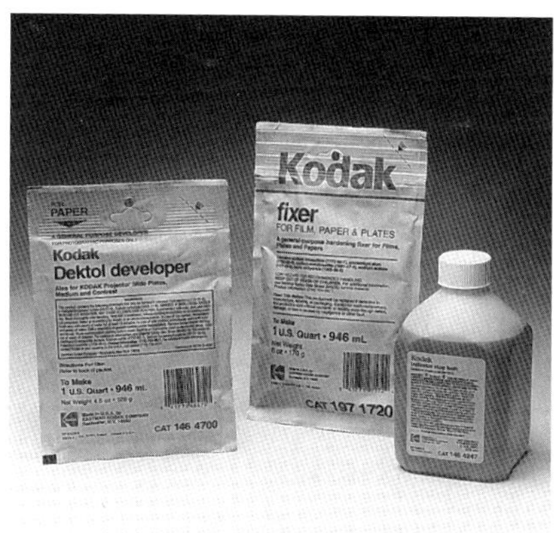

6 Chemicals: KODAK Developer, Fixer, and Stop Bath.

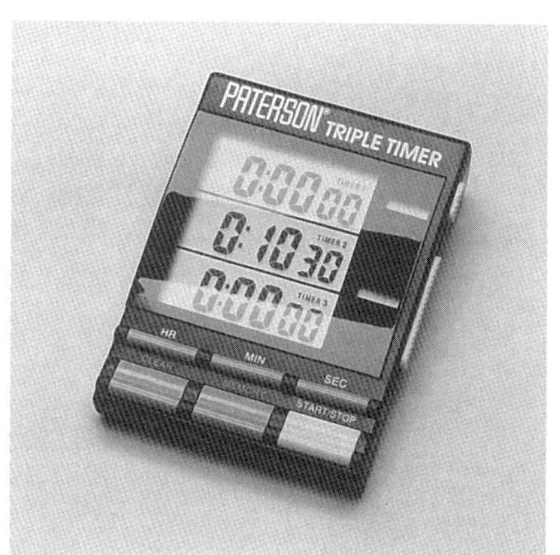

9 A darkroom timer or a clock with a sweep-second hand.

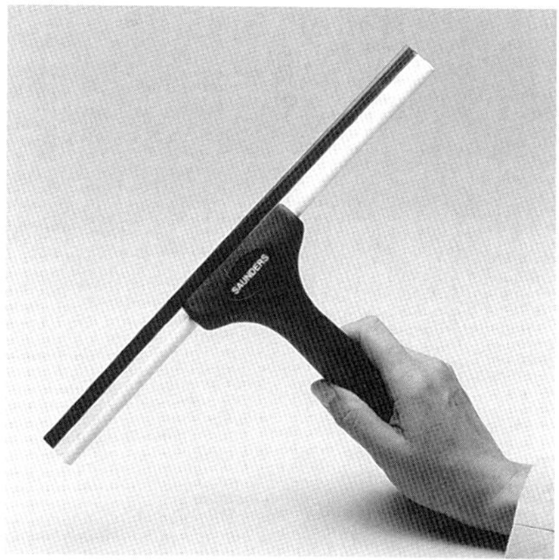

10 A sponge or a squeegee such as a Saunders or KODAK Rubber Squeegee.

Exposing and Processing the Proof Sheet

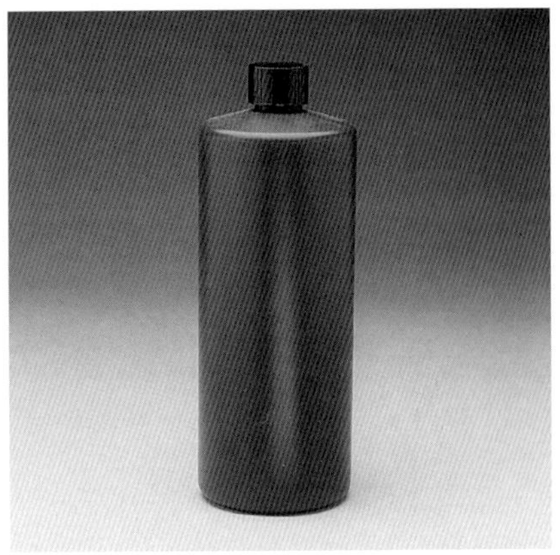

1 *In your 3 large bottles, mix the developer, stop bath, and fixer solutions according to the package instructions. Label the bottles PAPER DEVELOPER, STOP BATH, and FIXER.*

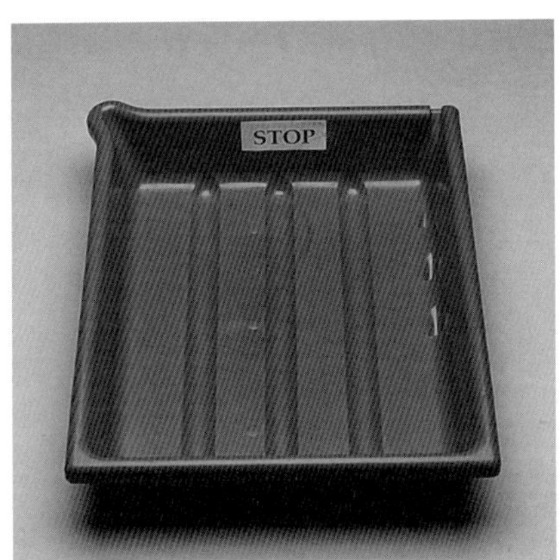

3 *Stabilize the stop bath at 65 to 75°F (18 to 24°C) and pour about 1/2 inch into a tray labeled STOP BATH or STOP.*

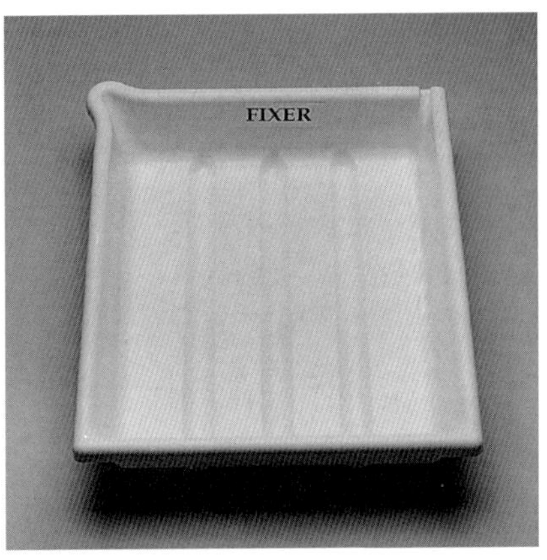

4 *Stabilize the fixer at 65 to 75°F (18 to 24°C) and pour about 1/2 inch into a tray labeled FIXER.*

TIP

Rinse your graduate after steps 2, 3, and 4.

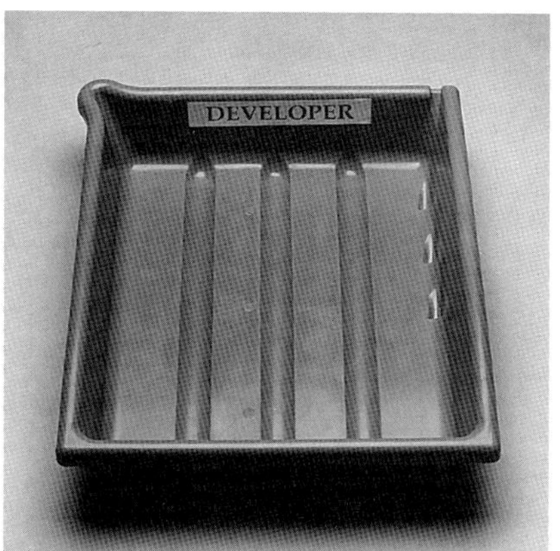

2 *Stabilize the developer at 68°F (20°C) by pouring about 32 oz (946 ml) into your graduate and placing it in a tray of cool or warm water. Next, pour it into a tray labeled DEVELOPER to a depth of about 1/2 inch.*

TIP

When handling or moving prints from tray to tray in steps 8-11, use print tongs or rubber gloves.

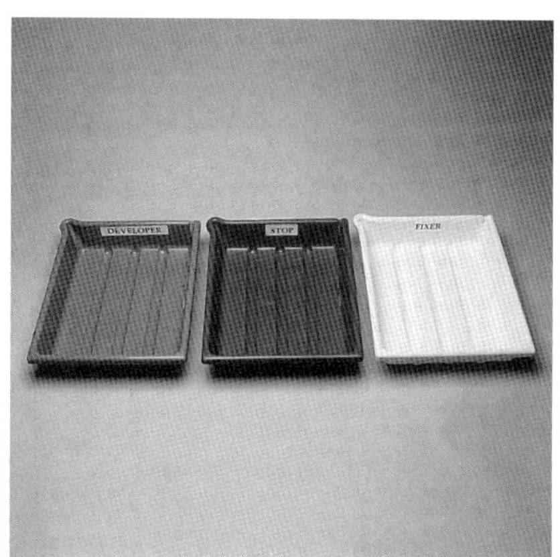

5 *Arrange your trays in front of you so that, from left to right, you have developer, stop bath, and fixer. Then rinse your hands well and dry them thoroughly. Turn off all lights except the safelight. The safelight should be placed at least 4 feet from your working area.*

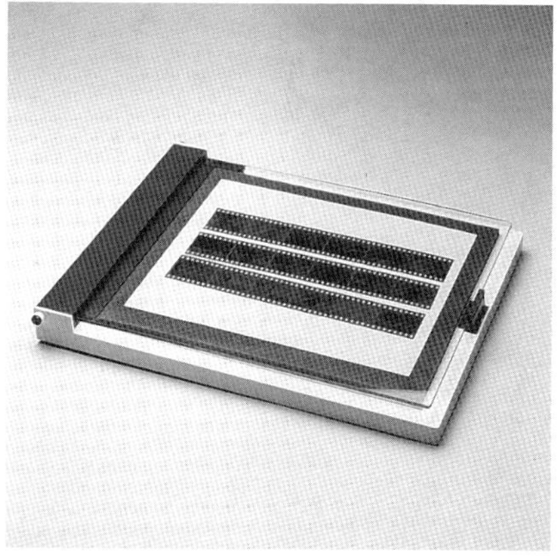

6 *Open the package of paper, remove one sheet, and close the package again so that light can't get in. Place your negatives so that their dull side faces the emulsion (usually shiny) side of the paper. Cover the paper and negatives with the glass. The negatives should be toward the light source.*

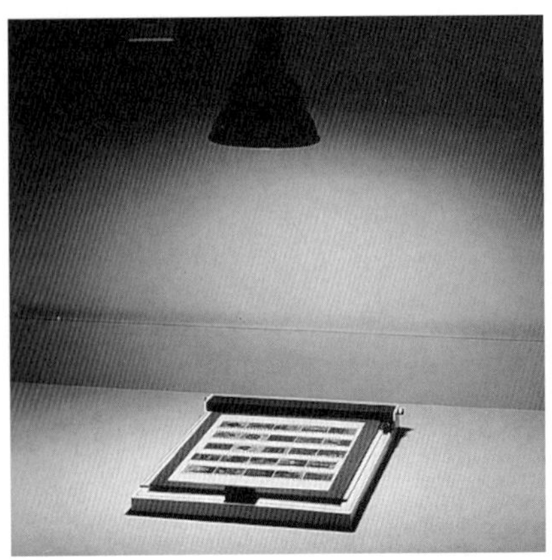

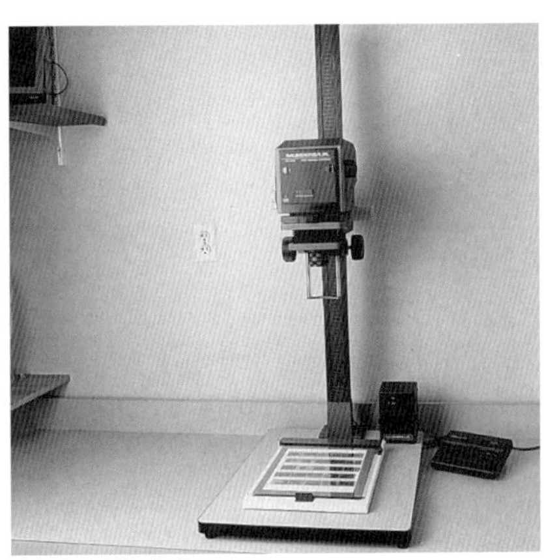

7 *If you're using a printing frame and a 7-watt bulb to make your proof sheet, hang the bare bulb 2 feet above the frame and turn it on for about 10 seconds. You may have to experiment a bit (see step 11) to get the correct exposure time for your negatives.*

If you're using an enlarger, place the empty negative carrier in the enlarger, and set the lens at f/11. Adjust the enlarger so that the light covers an area just a bit larger than your paper. Expose for about 8 seconds. Again, you may have to experiment to get the correct exposure time.

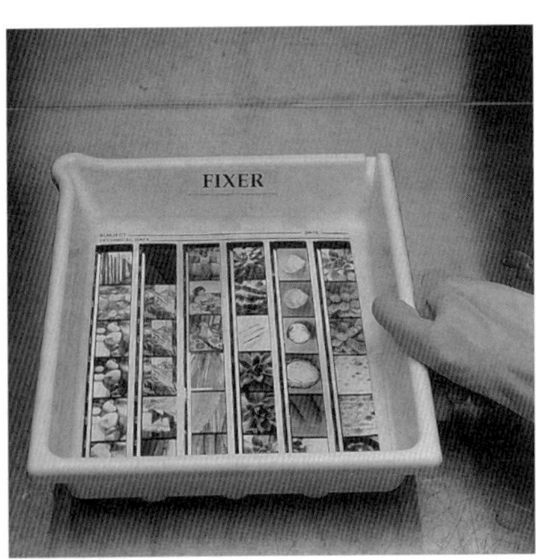

10 *With your right hand, withdraw the paper from the stop bath and slip it into the fixer. Agitate the paper frequently for 2 minutes. After the print has been in the fixer for 25 to 30 seconds, you can turn on the room lights.*

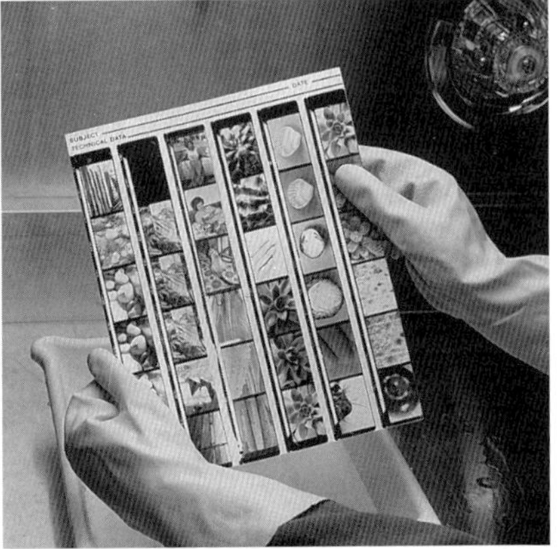

11 *Examine your proof sheet and if most of the pictures seem too light, try again with double the exposure time you used at first. If most of the pictures seem too dark, use half the exposure time. It's a good idea to keep notes on your exposure times and the results. You'll soon be able to come up with a good average exposure time to use.*

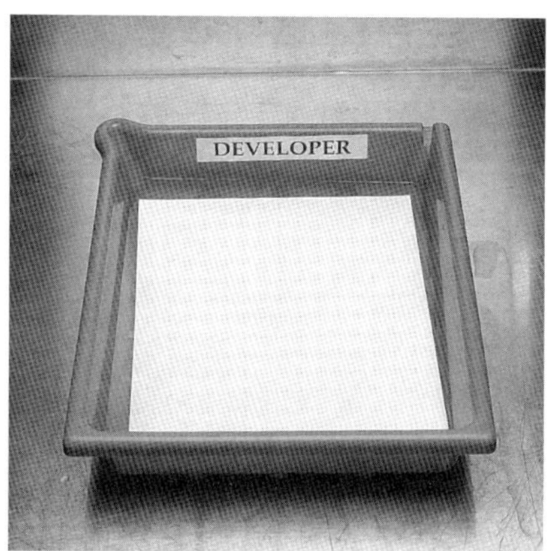

8 Remove the paper from your printing device with your left hand and slide the paper, emulsion side up, into the developer (left-hand tray). Don't get your right hand wet with developer. Rock the tray gently for 1 minute by tipping up first one end, then the other.

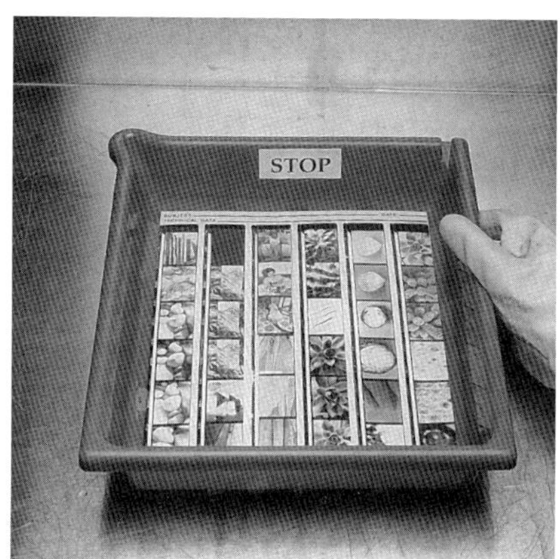

9 Take the paper out of the developer with your left hand, and after letting it drain for a second or two, slide it into the stop-bath solution (center tray). Agitate the tray for 10 seconds in the same manner you did in step 8.

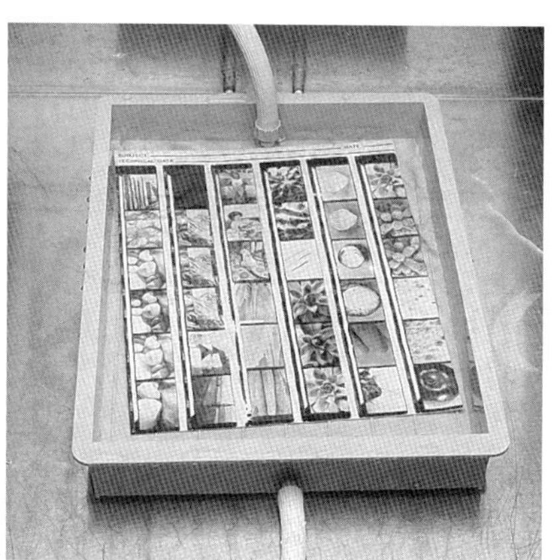

12 Using your fourth tray, wash the print for only 4 minutes at 65 to 75°F (18 to 24°C). The Paterson High-Speed Print Washer or the KODAK Automatic Tray Siphon provide continuous agitation.

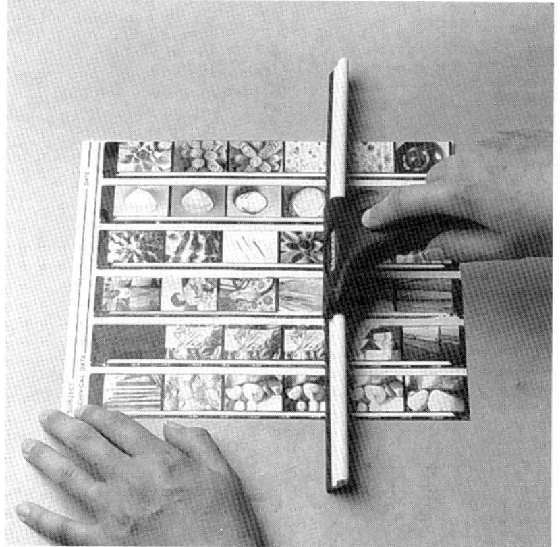

13 Sponge or squeegee the surface water from both sides of the print and place it on a flat surface to dry at room temperature.

Enlarging

You'll find a lot of satisfaction in making enlargements from your favorite black-and-white negatives. This chapter tells you how to go about it.

First of all, you'll need an enlarger. There are many kinds of enlargers, and your photo dealer will be glad to help you select one to suit your needs. Before continuing, be sure to become completely familiar with your enlarger. Read the instruction manual!

Before the negative goes into the enlarger, it has to be placed in a negative carrier. This is a glass or metal part that holds the negative in the enlarger. Light is passed through the negative and then directed by the enlarger lens onto an easel, which is a board that holds your paper.

Let's start out by enlarging one of the negatives you used for making your proof sheet. You'll do this in the same darkroom you used for contact printing, using the same safelight.

Things You'll Need

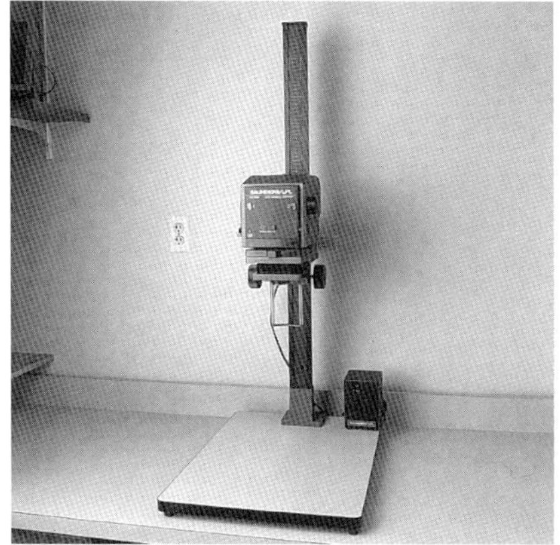

1 *An enlarger.*

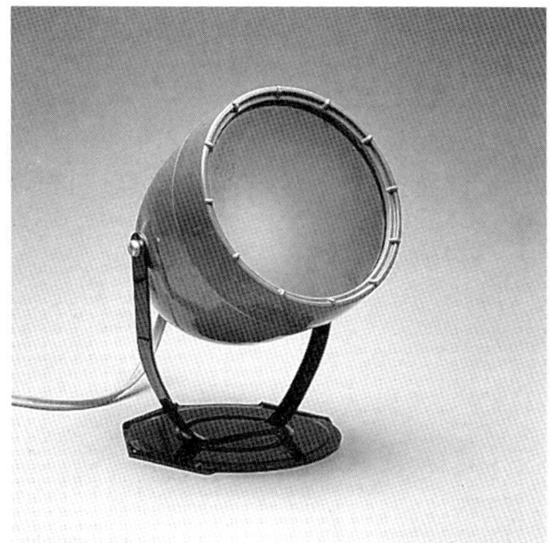

2 *The same safelight you used for contact printing.*

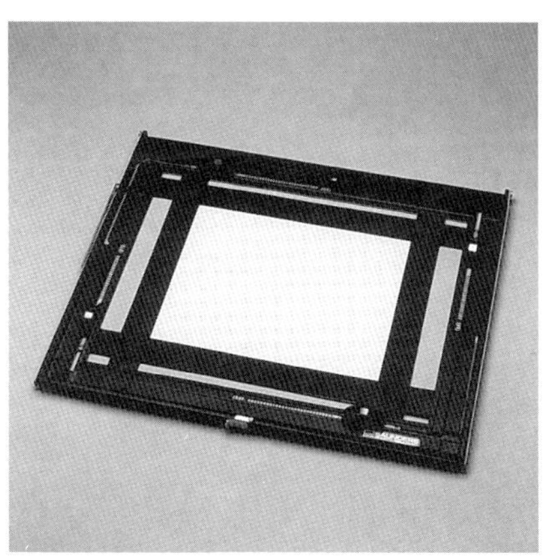

3 *An easel to hold the paper.*

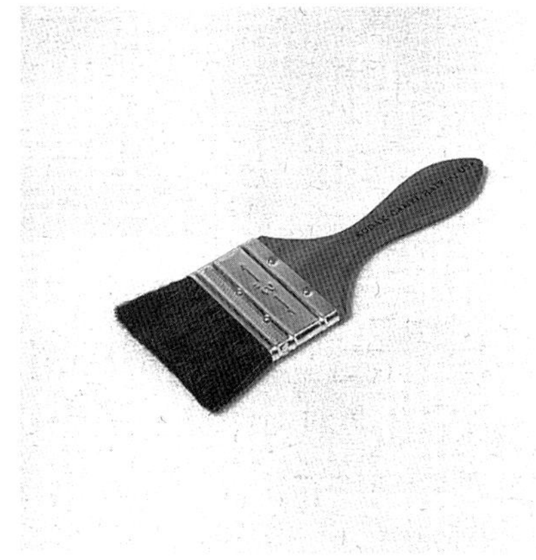

4 *A camel's-hair brush.*

Things You'll Need

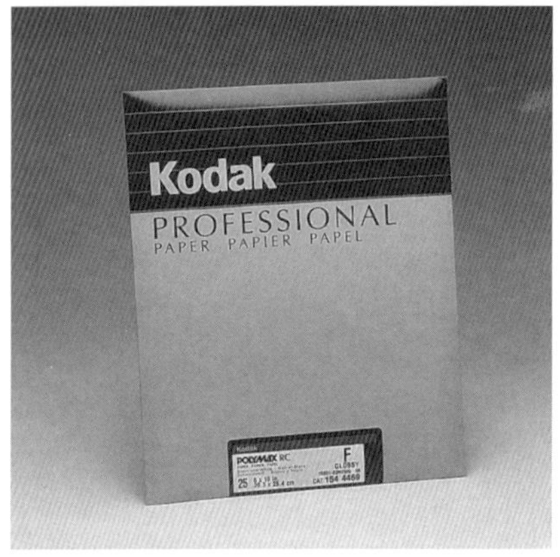

5 *The same KODAK POLYMAX RC Paper that you used to make a proof sheet.*

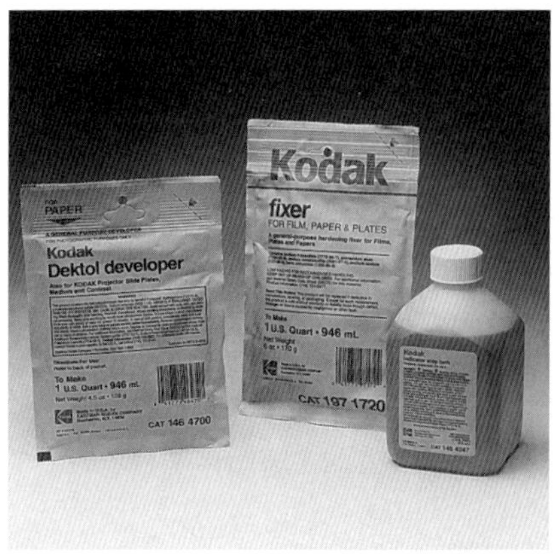

6 *The same chemicals you used to process your proof sheet. (For other chemicals, see page 65).*

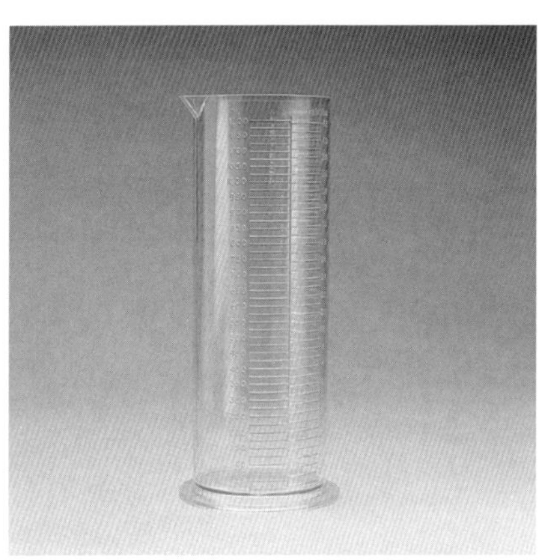

9 *A 42-ounce (1200 ml) graduate or kitchen measuring cup.*

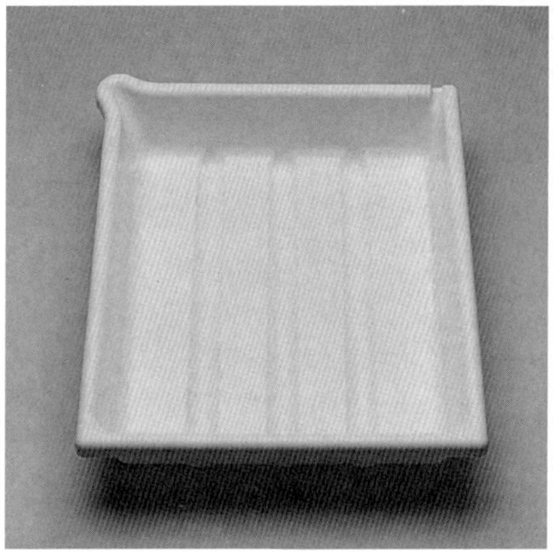

10 *The same trays you used when you made a proof sheet.*

Things You'll Need

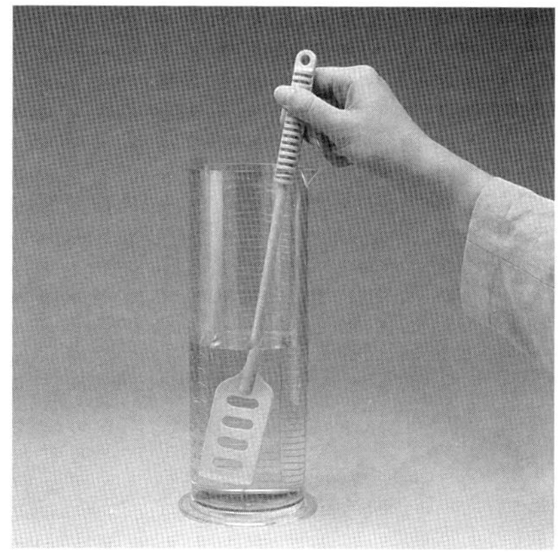

7 *A stirring rod to mix the chemicals.*

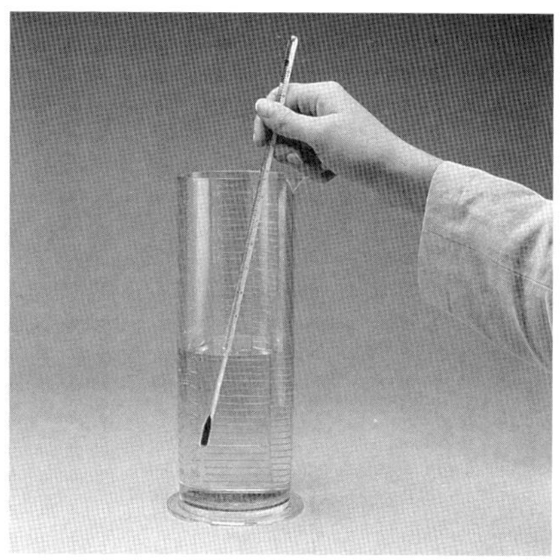

8 *A darkroom thermometer to measure solution temperatures.*

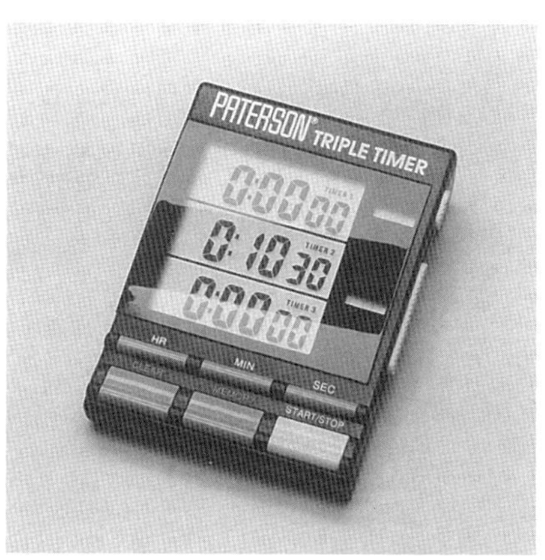

11 *A darkroom timer or a clock with a sweep-second hand.*

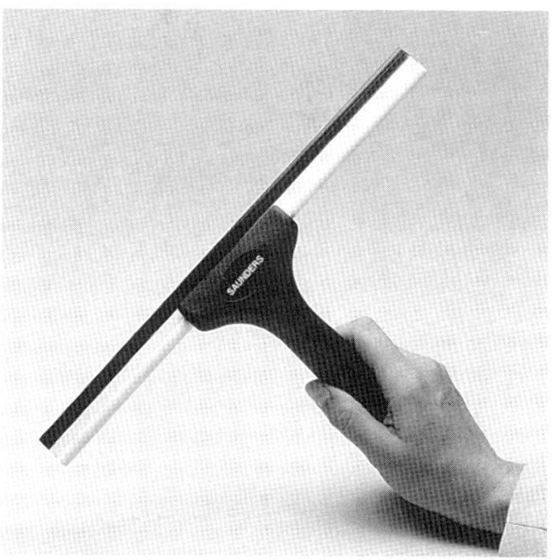

12 *A squeegee or sponge.*

Exposing and Processing the Enlargement

If you've already made a good proof sheet, you've had a good introduction to enlarging. The processing steps are nearly the same. And you'll be using the same chemicals you used for the proof sheet.

Enlarging is fun and rewarding, so let's get started!

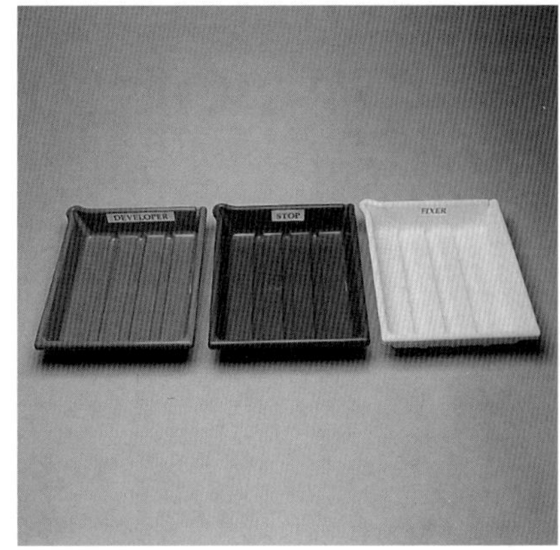

1 *Prepare your chemicals according to the instructions packaged with them. Put about 1/2 inch each of developer, stop bath, and fixer into 3 trays, just as you did when making a proof sheet.*

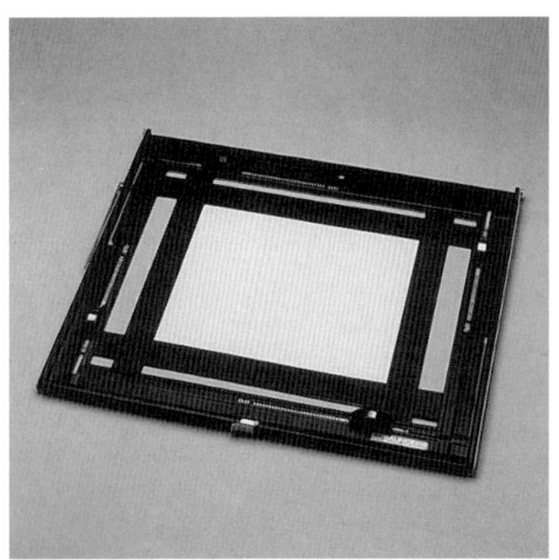

4 *Slide a sheet of smooth, white typing paper beneath the guides of the enlarger easel for a focusing aid; turn the safelight on and the room lights off. Wait a minute for your eyes to adjust.*

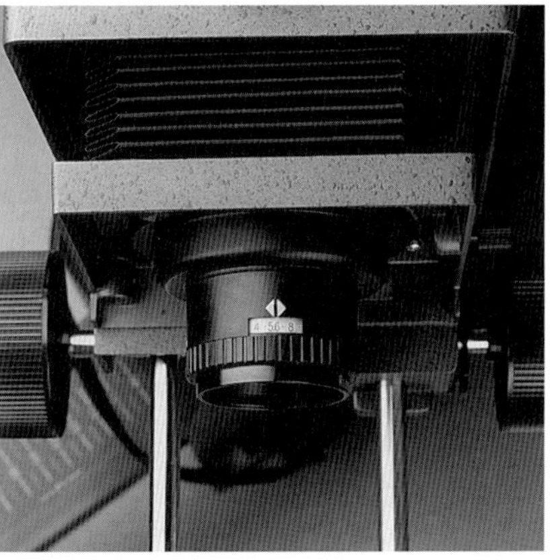

5 *Set the enlarger lens at its widest opening (the smallest number on the lens mount), and turn the enlarger on. By adjusting the height of the enlarger head, arrange your picture so that the negative image appears the way you want it within the easel guides.*

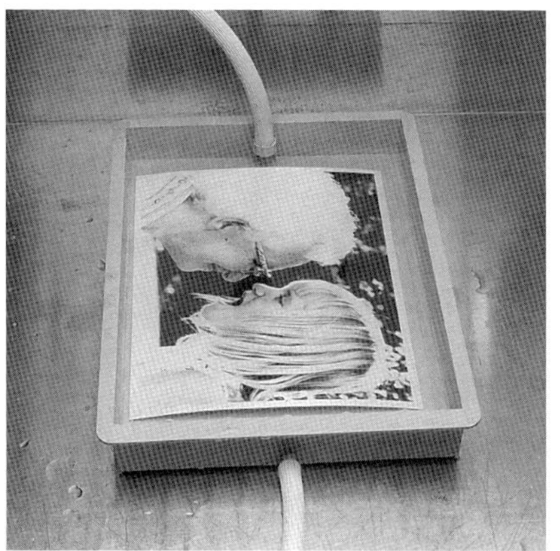

2 *Use a print washer or a fourth tray labeled WASH.*

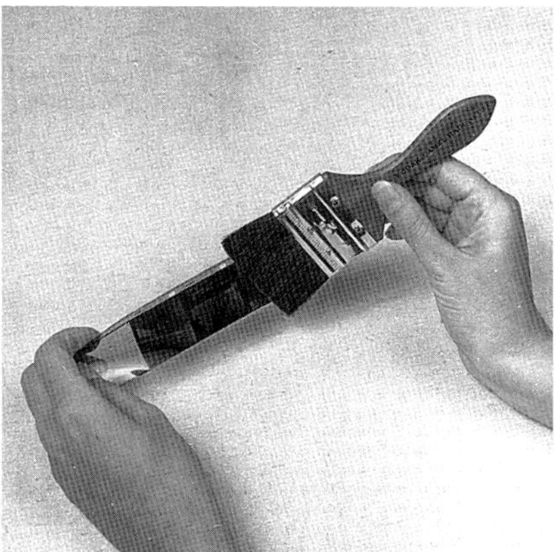

3 *Holding the negative gently by its edges, dust it on both sides with the camel's-hair brush. Select the correct negative carrier (dust it also if it's glass), and place your negative into it so that its emulsion side (that's the dull one) is down.*

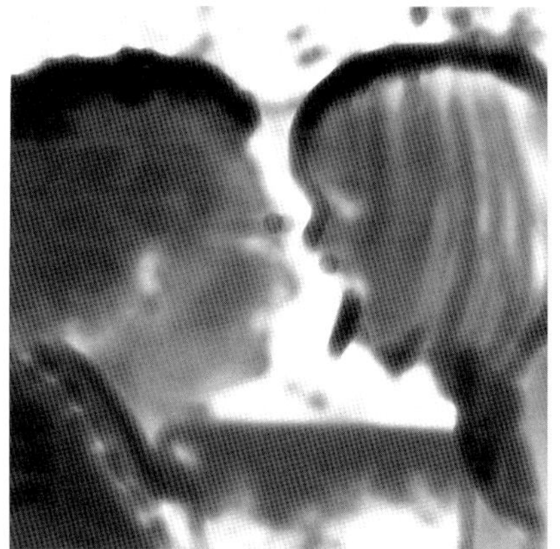

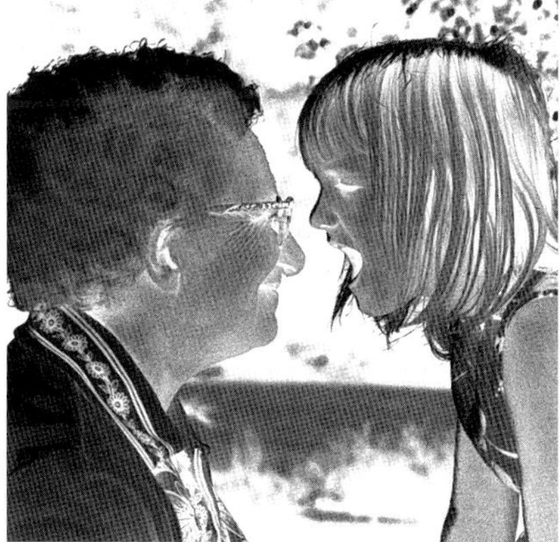

6 *By adjusting the enlarger lens, bring your picture into the sharpest possible focus. Then change the lens setting to f/11, and turn the enlarger off. Take a sheet of KODAK POLYMAX RC Paper and place it on the easel, emulsion side up.*

7 *Cover all but a sixth of this sheet with a piece of cardboard, and turn on the enlarger. Every 5 seconds, expose an additional sixth of the paper. At the end of 30 seconds, turn the enlarger off.*

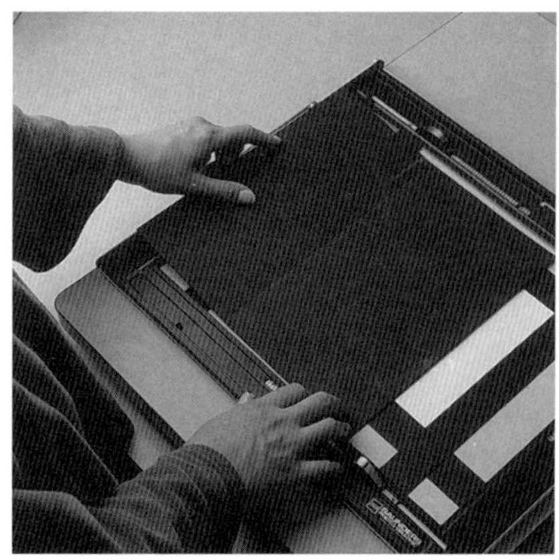

10 *Turn out the room lights, and put a piece of photographic paper, emulsion side up, onto the easel. Expose the paper and process it as you did the test print, but with a 2-minute fixing time. You can turn on the lights after 25 to 30 seconds. Wash the enlargement for only 4 minutes at 65 to 75°F (18 to 24°C). Use running water and agitate the print frequently while it is washing or use a print washer.*

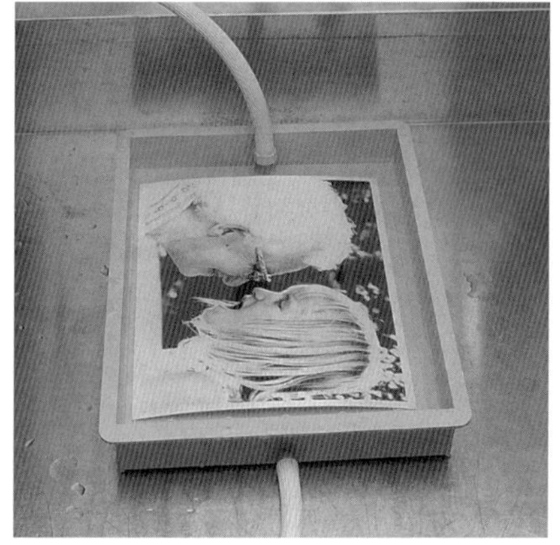

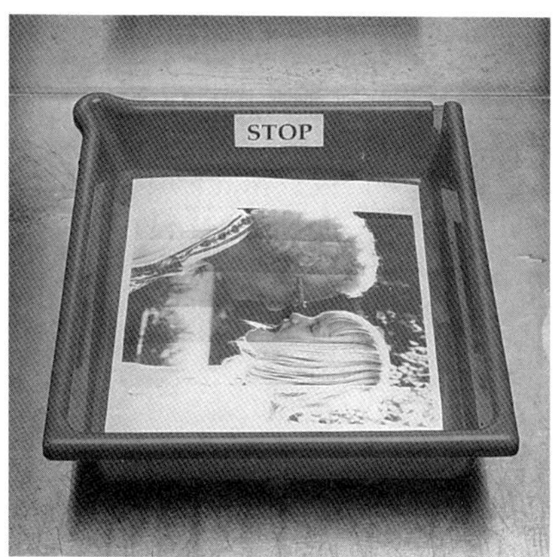

8 *Process this test sheet for 1 minute in the developer and 10 seconds in the stop bath; then slide it into the fixer for 25 to 30 seconds, and turn the room lights on.*

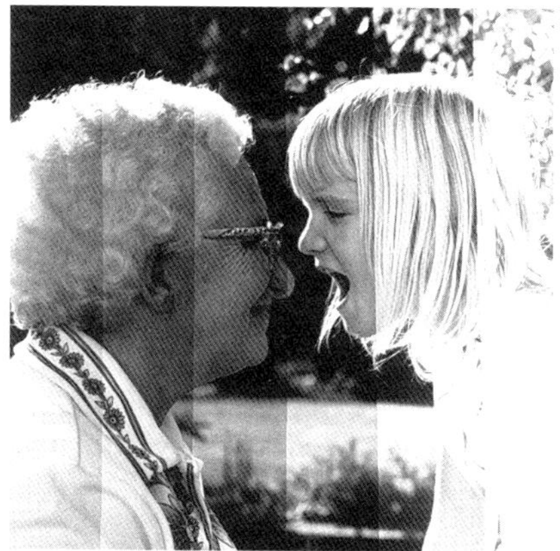

9 *From your print, choose the exposure time that gives the most pleasing result.*

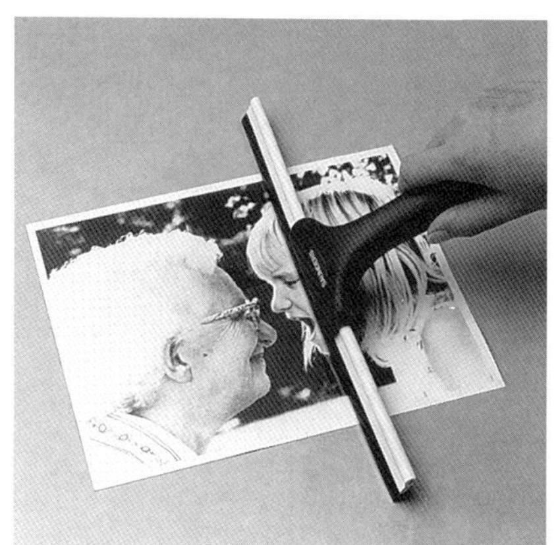

11 *Sponge or squeegee the surface water from both sides of the print, and place it on a flat surface to dry at room temperature.*

Evaluating the Print

After the print has been in the fixer for 25 to 30 seconds, you can turn on the room lights and examine your print. If you have a print made by a photofinisher, compare the two. Is yours too light? Too dark? If your print looks too light, make another with double the exposure. If the print is too dark, cut the exposure time in half.

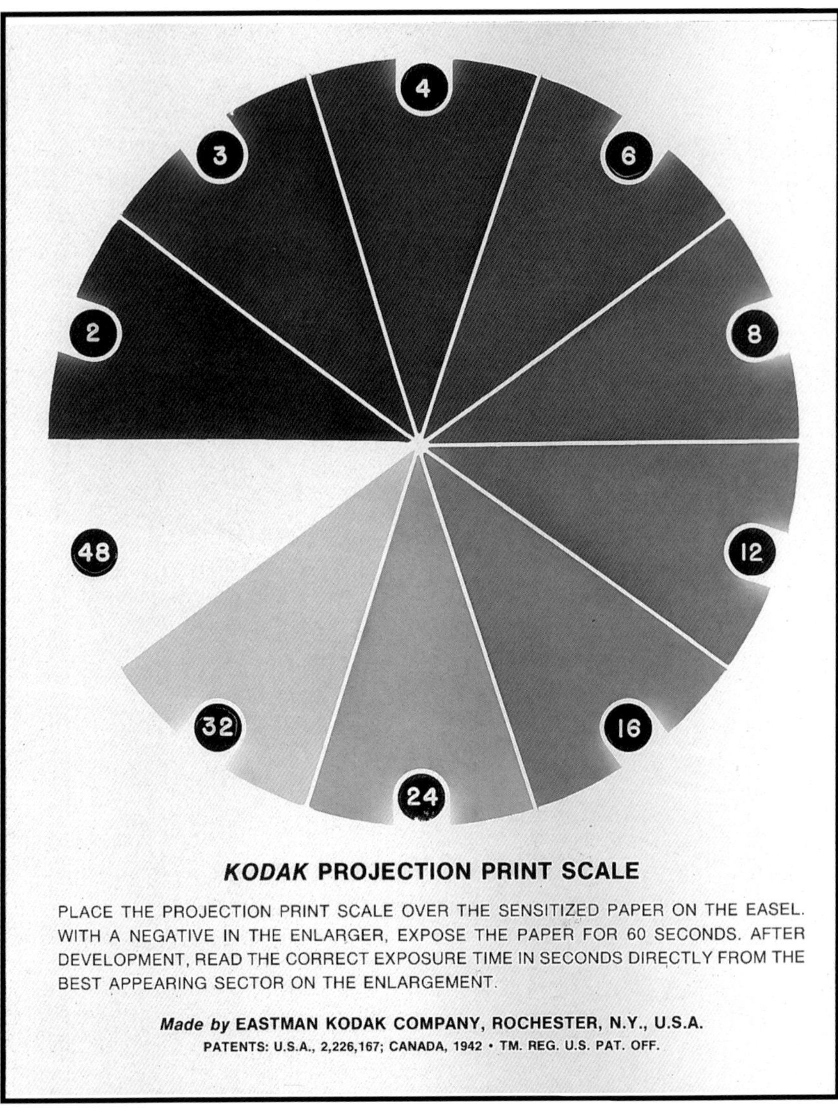

Actual Size

KODAK Projection Print Scale

Now you've made an enlargement. Remember the method you used to find the right exposure—making a test print of different exposure times? Well there's an easier way to do it. The KODAK Projection Print Scale is a piece of film divided like a pie, with a number in each of its 10 slices. To use it, you focus the negative, turn off the enlarger, and place a piece of enlarging paper on the easel. Place the print scale so that it reads correctly on top of the paper. Turn on the enlarger for exactly 1 minute with the lens set at *f*/11. Then process the paper. Pick the section of the pie that looks best. The number in that section will be the exposure time in seconds.

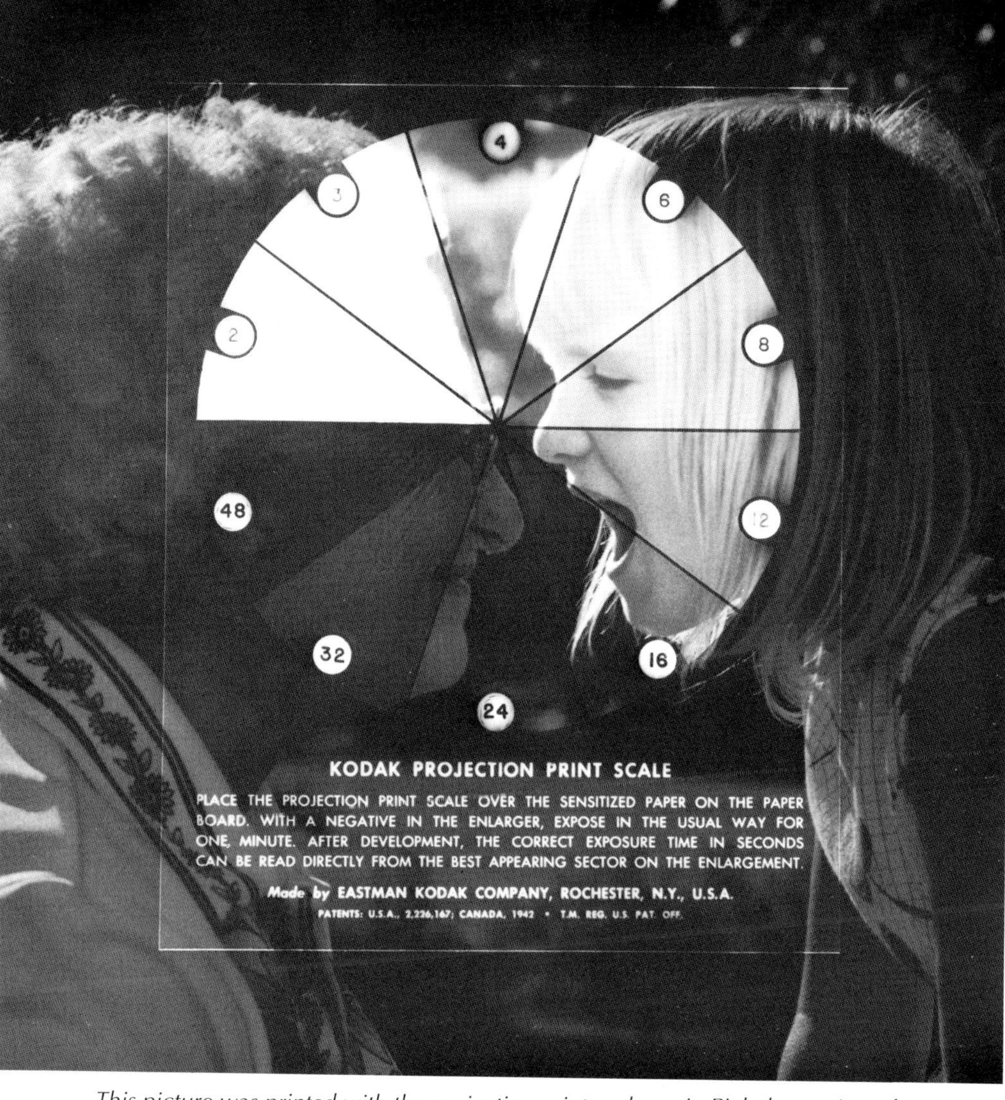

This picture was printed with the projection print scale on it. Pick the section of the scale that looks best. The number in that section will be the exposure time in seconds. In this case, the exposure would be 8 or 12 seconds, depending on your preference.

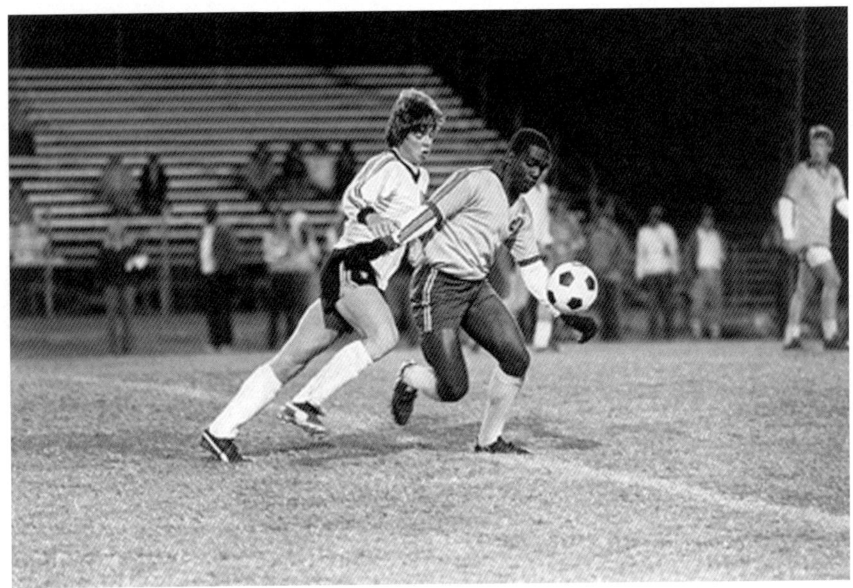

You can improve many pictures by printing only the best part of the scene. The picture on the right has a lot more impact than the one above. A lot of the background was cropped out to make a close-up that emphasizes the intense competition between the two players.

Enlarging Parts of Negatives

Although you enlarged the whole negative when you made your first enlargement, you may want to enlarge only a part of the negative. You can improve many pictures by printing only the best part of the scene, eliminating cluttered backgrounds or unimportant areas. This is called cropping.

Suppose, for example, that your negative is a full-length picture of a person. If you like, you can enlarge just the small area of the negative containing the image of the person's head. When enlarging only part of a negative, be sure to use more exposure time than you did when enlarging the whole negative.

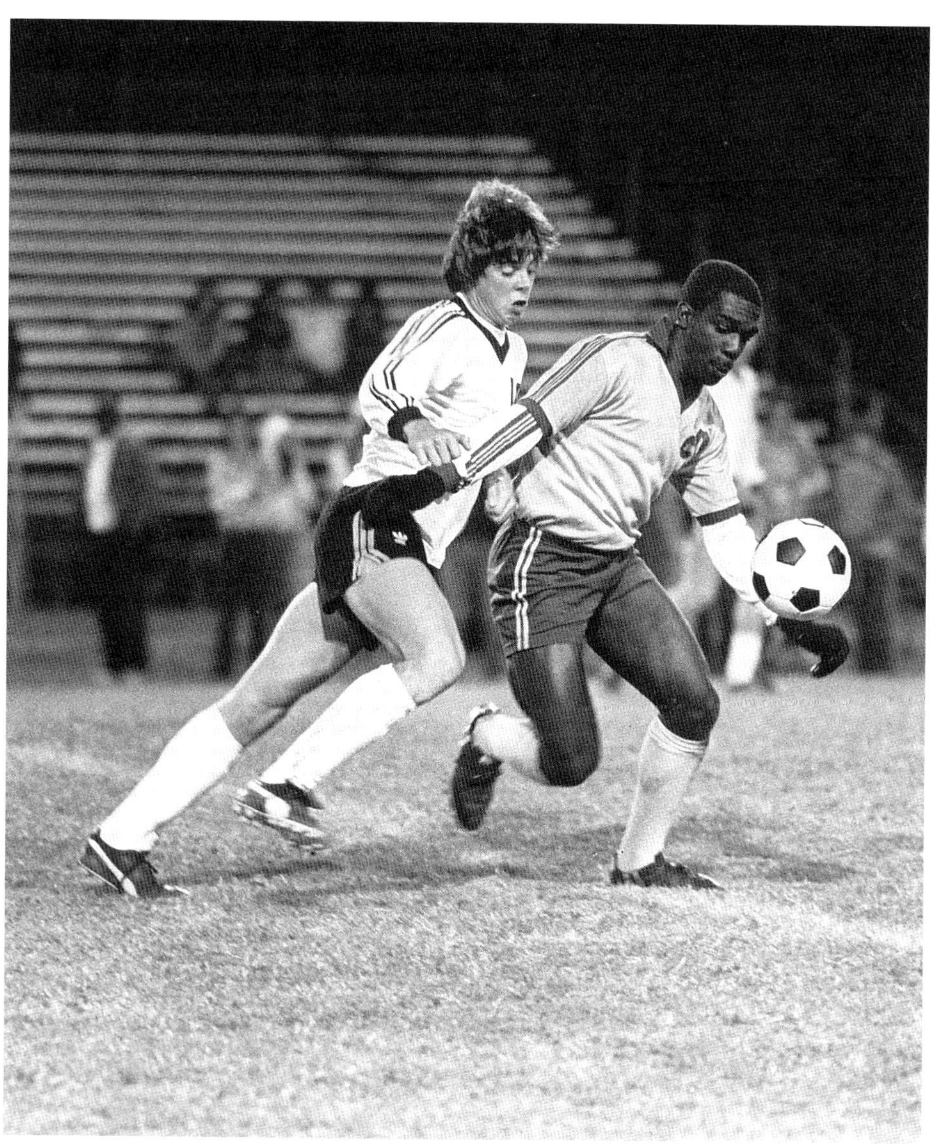

The photo was cropped to isolate the subject and improve the overall composition.

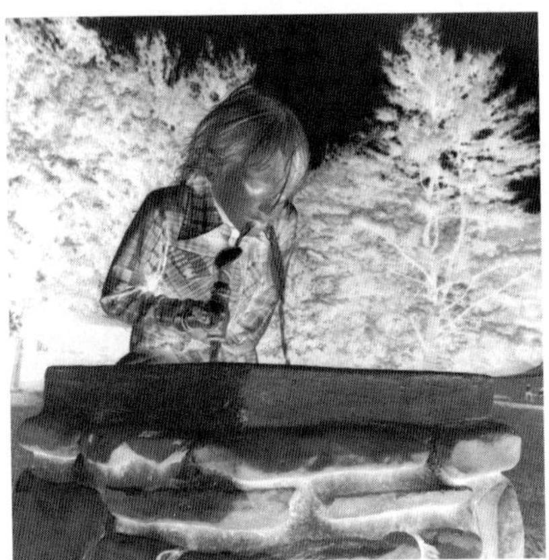

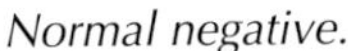

Normal negative.

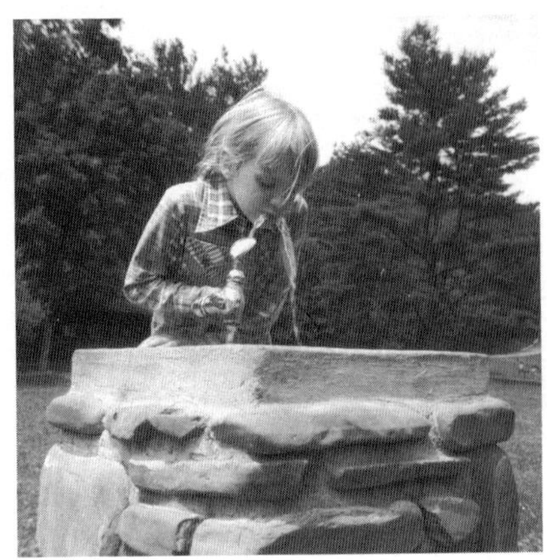

A print made with a No. 1 filter is flat.

Now Try This

KODAK POLYCONTRAST III RC Paper is a selective-contrast paper. When exposed with KODAK POLYMAX Filters, this paper can have 12 different degrees of contrast.

When exposed without filters, KODAK POLYCONTRAST III RC Paper is for normal negatives. Flat, low-contrast negatives need a No. 3 or 4 filter to make good prints. Contrasty negatives, on the other hand, should be printed with a No. 1 or 0 filter. You might try printing some of your own flat or contrasty negatives with the correct filter. Different types of negatives are illustrated here to help you see what they look like.

The KODAK POLYMAX Filter Set contains 12 filters that enable you to vary the contrast range of Kodak selective-contrast papers in half-step intervals from Grade -1 to Grade 5+. For more information on contrast grades, see page 61.

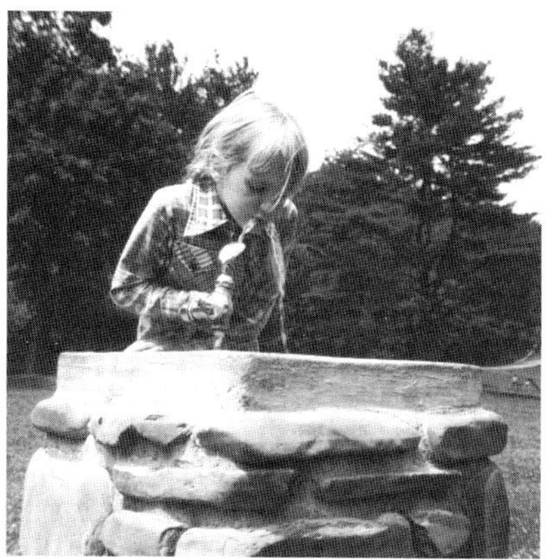

A print made without a filter or with a No. 2 filter looks good.

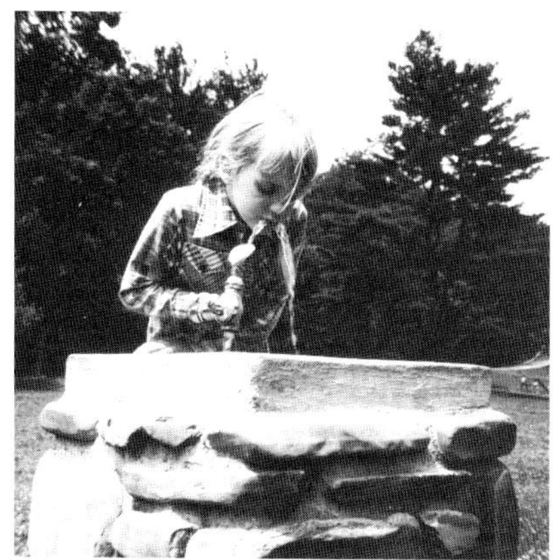

A print made with a No. 4 filter is contrasty.

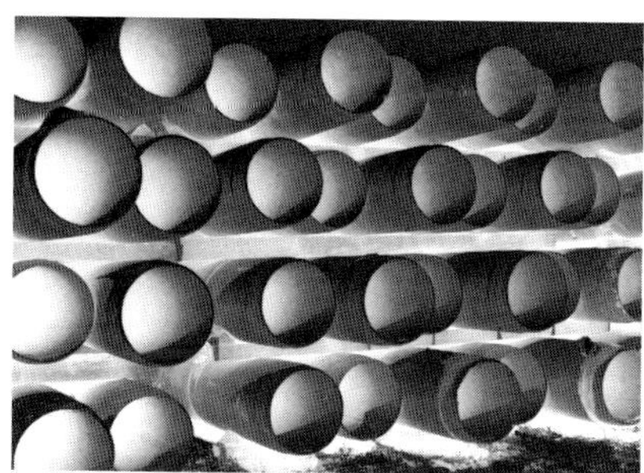

Contrasty negative.

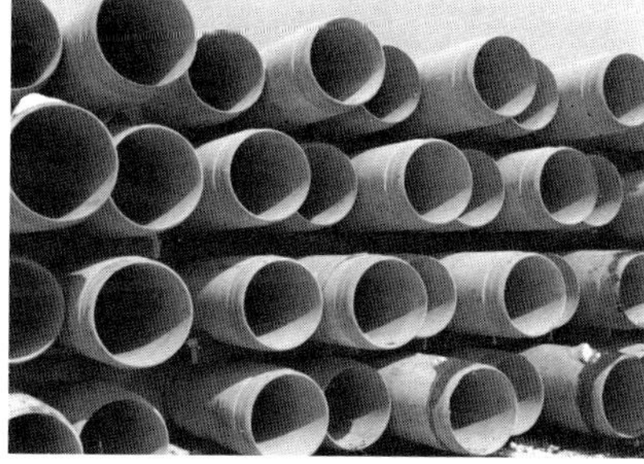

No. 1 filter.

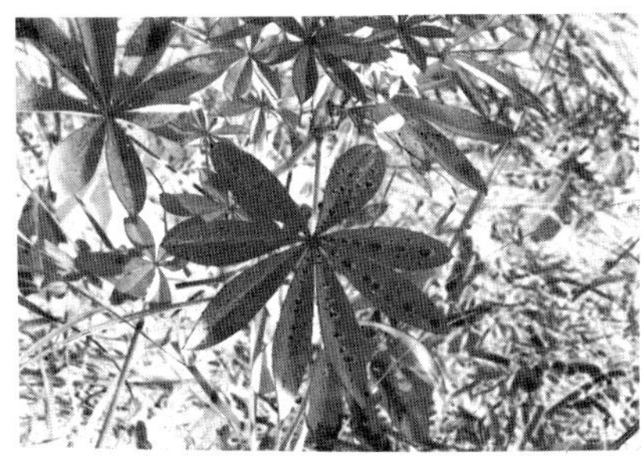

Low-contrast negative.

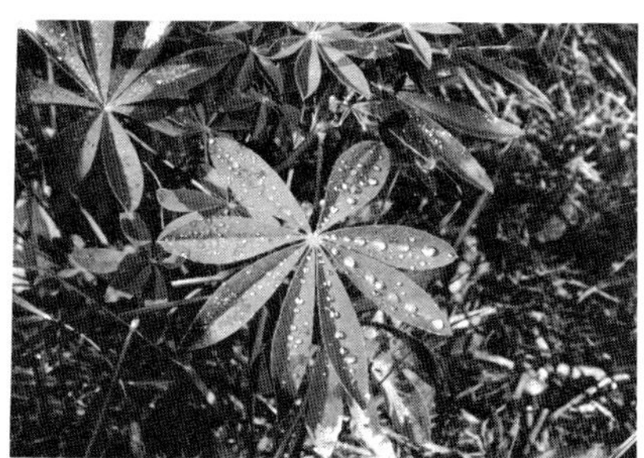

No. 4 filter.

Control Techniques

Up until now we've been concerned primarily with making straight enlargements—enlargements made without the use of any special control techniques. However, using control techniques, along with print-finishing techniques (see page 44), often makes the difference between a good print and an excellent one. Of course, not all negatives require special printing treatment. But since control techniques are quite useful, this section will cover some of the most important controls, such as dodging and burning-in. These are the tools you can use to produce high-quality enlargements.

Composition

Composition means the arrangement of the lines and areas that make up your picture. While entire books have been written on composition, there are a few basic pointers that will help you compose the most pleasing and interesting enlargement. For example, it's usually better not to have the center of interest in the middle of the picture or too near the margins. Also, try to keep the horizon line in scenic shots above or below the midpoint of the picture, rather than dividing the picture in the middle.

Your picture should tell its story as simply and clearly as possible. This means you should try to eliminate areas and details that are unnecessary or distracting. Often you can do this simply by shifting the enlarger easel. Or perhaps you can enlarge the picture more, to eliminate distracting areas near the edges.

If your picture contains a light area that draws attention away from the main subject or an area that would print too dark, you may be able to correct this by burning-in or dodging.

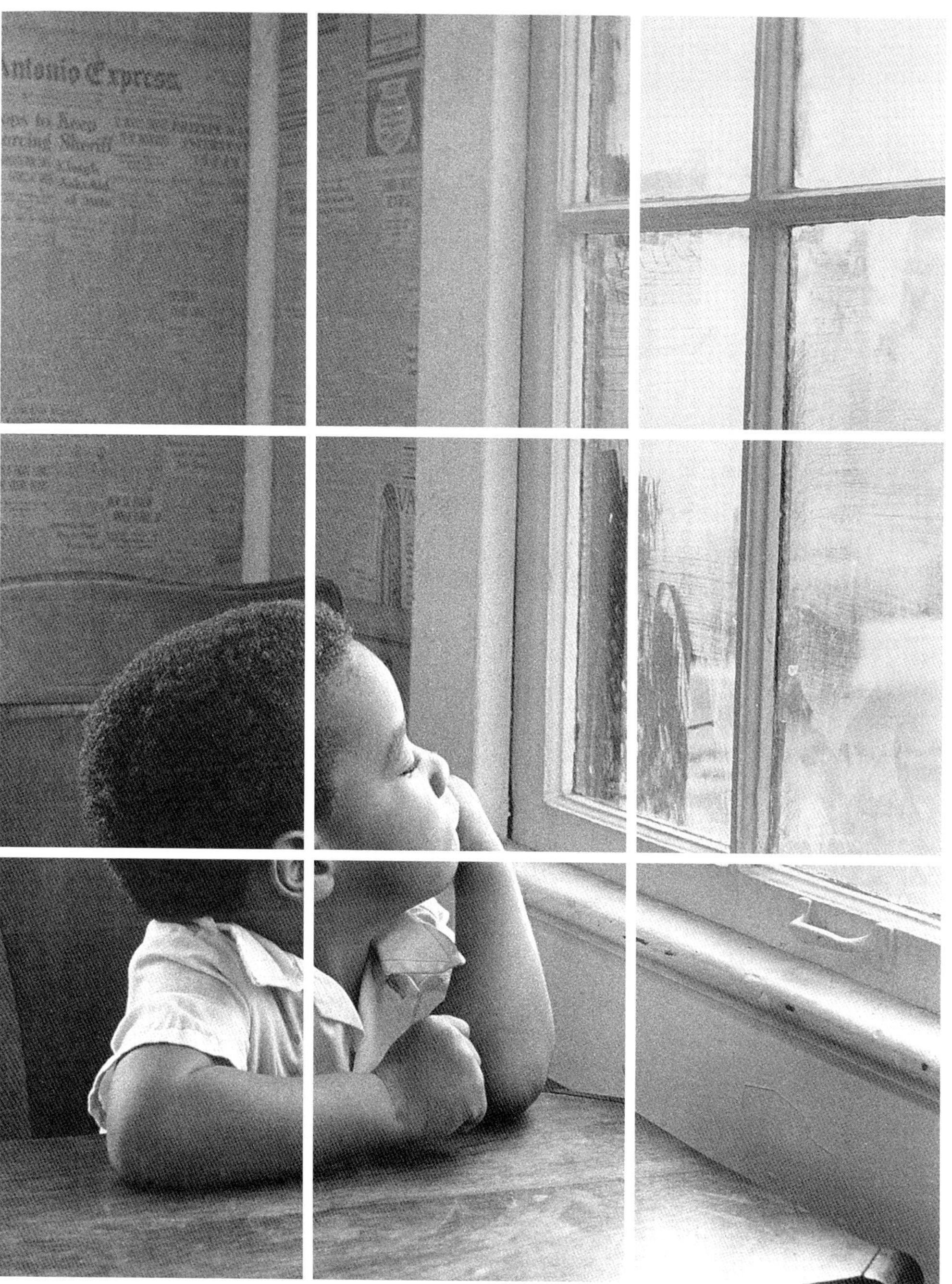

When composing your picture, you may want to follow the rule of thirds. Divide your picture area into thirds, both vertically and horizontally. Place your center of interest at one of the four places where the lines intersect.

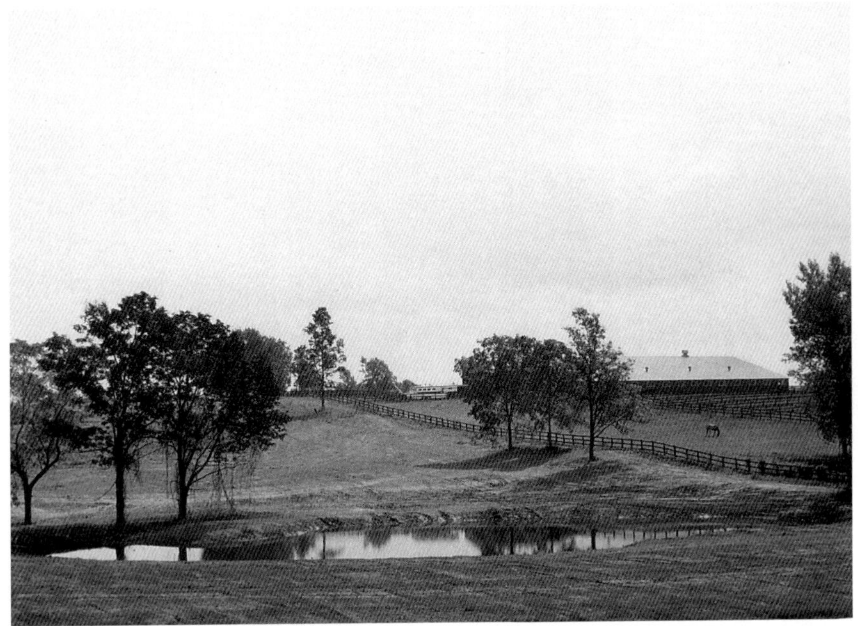

There are many situations where burning-in comes in handy. In the picture above, the clouds are rather weak and washed-out. Burning-in darkens them and makes them more dramatic in the picture on the right.

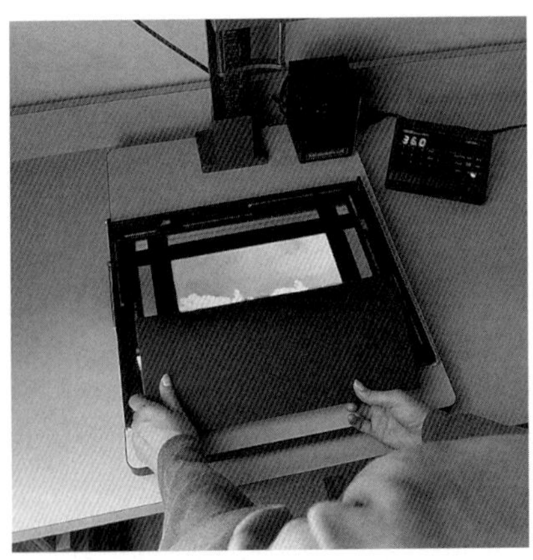

After you've given the paper a normal exposure, hold a piece of cardboard under the enlarger lens about midway between the lens and the paper. Turn on the enlarger, and move the cardboard so that only the area of the image that is too light receives additional exposure.

Burning and Dodging

In many instances, the brightness range of a subject is far beyond the range of tones that can be reproduced in a print. However, you can partially compensate for this in two ways: (1) You can give additional exposure to the highlight areas that would otherwise print too light. This is called burning-in or printing-in. (2) You can hold light back from areas that would otherwise print too dark. This is called dodging.

You can easily make your own burning-in and dodging tools from wire, black tape, and dark paper or cardboard. When you use these tools, always keep them moving so that you won't be able to see a sharp line on the finished print, indicating where you burned-in or dodged.

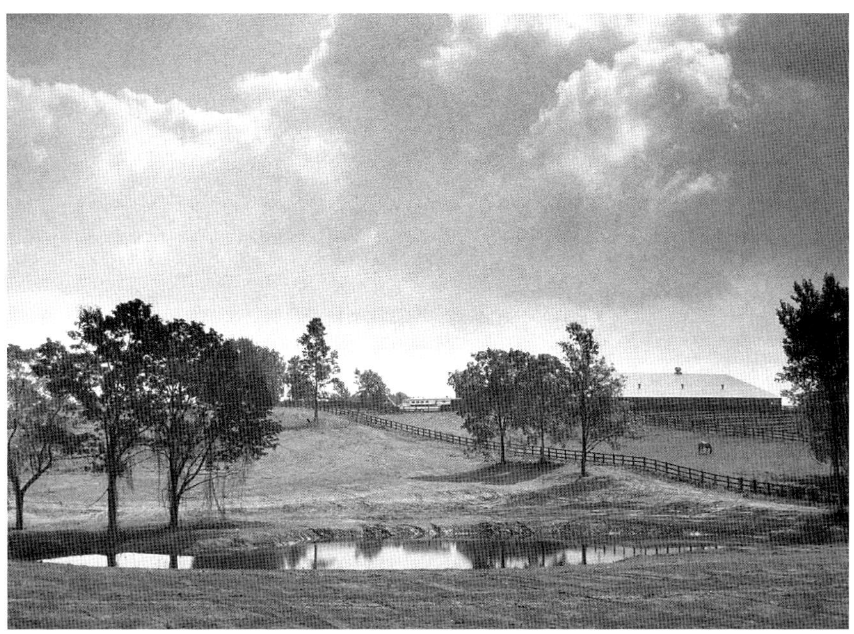

Burning-In

There are many situations where burning-in comes in handy. For example, let's assume you've taken a flash picture of a group of people. When you make a straight print from the negative, the people in the foreground will probably be much lighter than those who were farther from the camera. You can darken the people in the foreground by burning-in. After you've given the print its normal exposure, hold a piece of cardboard under the enlarger lens about midway between the lens and the paper. Turn on the enlarger and move the cardboard so that only the area of the image that is too light receives additional exposure. If the area you want to darken is small or near the center of the paper, it's easier to confine the additional exposure to that area if you do the burning-in with a piece of cardboard in which you've cut a hole. Remember to keep the cardboard in continuous motion so that the doctoring won't be apparent on the finished print.

A technically good print of a landscape that reproduces all the tones in the original scene may be weakened pictorially by light-toned areas that compete for attention with the center of interest. These light areas could be bright stones in the foreground, bright reflections, a white house, a light sky, or some other distracting element. You can darken such areas by burning-in.

If the line between the satisfactory area and the area you want to darken is rather intricate, you can make a burning-in tool from a test print of the same size. Just cut the area you want to darken out of the test print. After you've given your final print its normal exposure, burn in the area that is too light by holding the cutout print very close to the paper you are exposing. Move the cutout print only very slightly during the exposure.

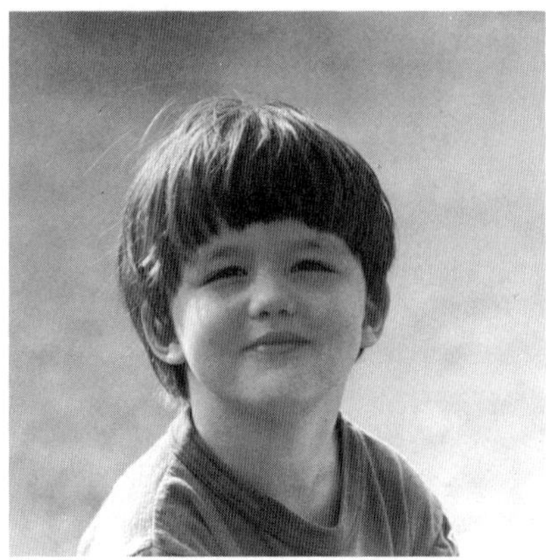

This is the original picture. The boy's face is filled with shadows.

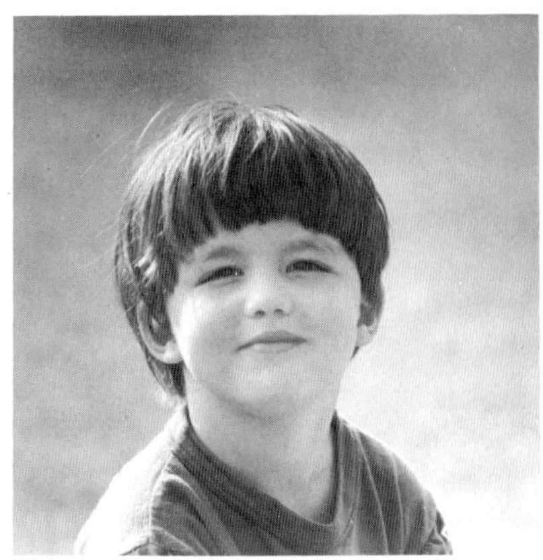

Dodging helps eliminate some of the shadows and make the boy's face lighter.

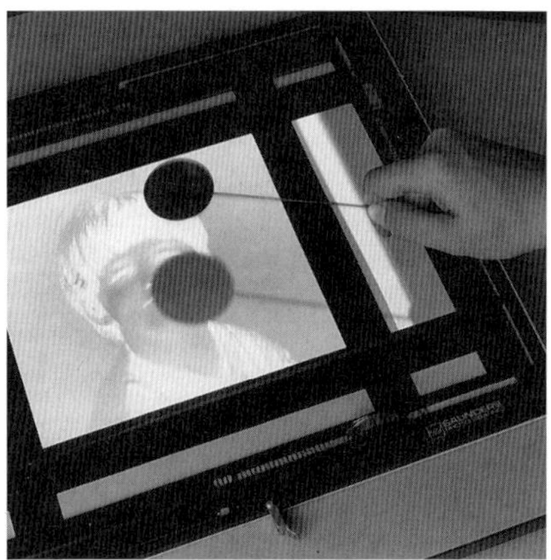

While you expose the print, hold the cardboard by the wire and move it over the area of the projected image that is too dark.

Dodging

In dodging, you hold back light from the projected image during the basic exposure time so that the photographic paper receives less-than-normal exposure in areas that were too dark in your straight print. The tools used in dodging are also very simple to make. You can cut any shape you need from a piece of dark cardboard or paper, and tape it to a piece of wire. Then while you expose the print, hold the cardboard over the area of the projected image that is too dark. In dodging, besides keeping the cardboard in motion, make sure you move the wire from side to side too. Otherwise you can get a light line on your print caused by the shadow of the wire.

Vignetting

Vignetting is a print technique used to eliminate distracting or unwanted backgrounds. This technique is used primarily in enlargements of people. Vignetting is most popular for printing high-key portraits—portraits of a subject made up of mostly light gray tones.

You can easily vignette a print by projecting the image from the negative through a hole in an opaque cardboard. Cut the hole in the cardboard the same shape as the area you want to print. The hole should be the size that will give you the effect you want when you hold the cardboard about halfway between the enlarger lens and the paper. Feather or rough-

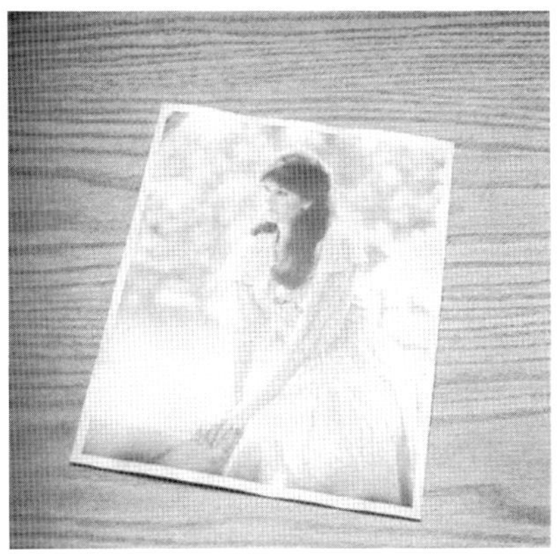

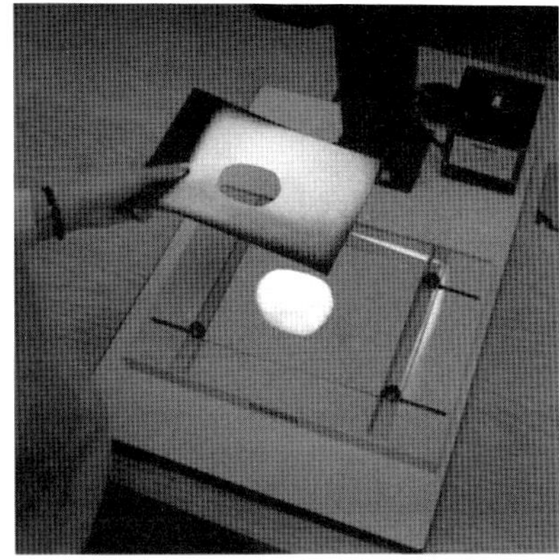

A vignette eliminates distracting backgrounds. The easiest tool for producing one is a piece of cardboard with an oval hole cut in it.

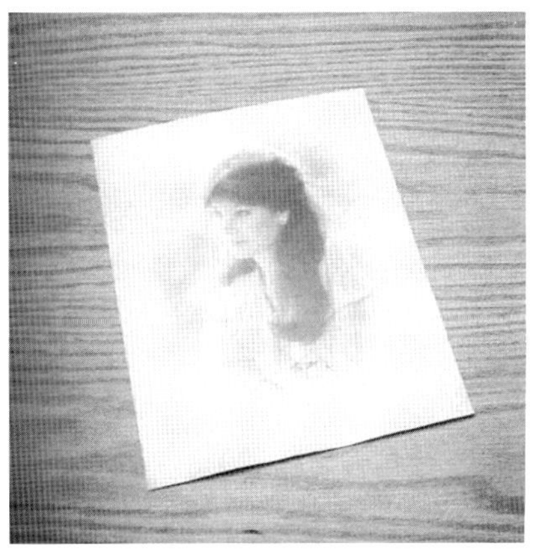

cut the edges of the hole so that the image fades gradually into the white paper. In vignetting, keep the vignetter in continuous motion during the print exposure.

You can use the vignetting technique to print portraits from more than one negative on a single sheet of enlarging paper. Assume you want to print from three negatives. Decide where you want each image to appear on the final print, and draw circles on a sheet of white paper on the enlarger easel to indicate the location of each image. Put the first negative in the enlarger and adjust it so that the image you want fills its circle. Remove the white sheet of paper and make your exposure test for the first negative. It isn't necessary to use the vignetting technique for your exposure test. Using the vignetting technique, make the first exposure on the enlarging paper that will be your final print. (It's a good idea to put a small "x" in one corner on the back of the enlarging paper to help keep it properly oriented.) After you make the exposure, put the sheet of enlarging paper back into its lighttight storage place. Put the paper with the circles on it back into the easel and adjust the enlarger for the second picture. Follow the same procedure as you did for the first negative. After you've printed the second negative, follow this same procedure for the third negative. Then process the print.

Print Finishing

After you've processed your enlargement, there are a number of finishing techniques you can use to add the final touch that can set your enlargement apart from others. This section describes some of those techniques.

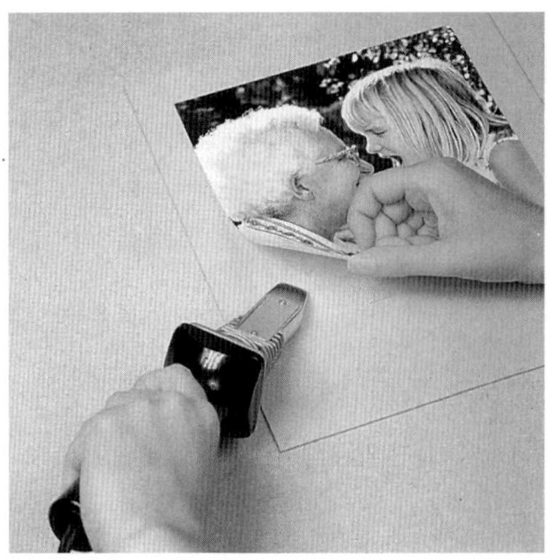

Holding the print in place, lift one corner and tack the mounting tissue to the mount. Do this on three corners.

Mounting

A mount dissociates a picture from its surroundings and therefore emphasizes the picture. Usually a special mounting board is used for this purpose. A well-chosen mount directs attention to the picture, not to itself. Many photographers use a material such as KODAK Dry Mounting Tissue, Type 2, for mounting their prints. Here's how to mount a print:

1. Tack the heat-sensitive tissue to the center of the back of the print, using a tacking iron or a household iron. (Set the household iron at the lowest setting in the synthetic-fabrics range and adjust if necessary.)
2. Trim the print and position it on the mounting board. Holding the print in place, lift one corner of the print and tack the mounting tissue to the mount. Tack two more corners.
3. If you plan to use a dry-mounting press, be sure to protect the print with a double thickness of heavy kraft wrapping paper. Before you put your print into the press, make sure that the kraft paper is completely dry. Close the press on the kraft paper for about 1 minute. This will keep the paper from sticking to the surface of your print. Place your covered print in the press and close the press for at least 30 seconds. The temperature of the press should be between 180 and 210°F (82 and 99°C).
4. Remove the mounted print from the press, place the print face-down on a clean, smooth surface, and keep it flat until it is cool. A heavy book or other flat weight is useful for this purpose.
5. If you don't have a mounting press, you can use a household iron to do your mounting. Use the same setting on the iron as suggested for tacking the mounting tissue to the print (see step 1). Cover the print with a double thickness of kraft paper, and run the iron back and forth over the print. Keep the iron moving, and work from the center of the print toward the edges. Don't push down too hard or you could mar the surface of the print.

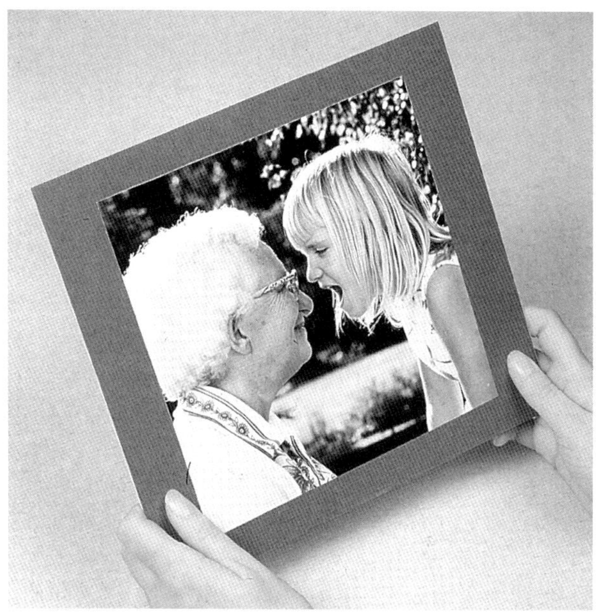

Underlays in gray, black, or color dress up a print.

Underlays in gray, black, or color dress up a print. Here's how to mount a print with an underlay.

1. Tack the dry-mounting tissue to the print, and trim off the excess tissue.
2. Tack the print to a piece of art paper that is slightly larger than the print. Do this just as you would to tack the print to a mounting board.
3. Tack dry-mounting tissue to the art paper, and trim the excess tissue.
4. Tack the art paper to the mounting board.
5. Mount the print with a mounting press or a household iron.

Other materials are also available for "cold" mounting at room temperature. Cold mounting is similar to mounting with dry-mounting tissue, but you don't need to apply heat to seal the print to the mounting board.

Products for cold mounting are pressure-sensitive, double-sided adhesives that you position on the print and roll or squeegee to bond the adhesive to the print. After you remove the attached liner, you bond the other side to the mounting board by rolling or squeegeeing.

Another way to mount prints is to use overlay mounts. You can buy overlay mounts in art- or photo-supply stores. There's no actual mounting involved when you use an overlay. Just lift the overlay and slide the print into place. Then tape or glue the bottom corners of the print to the mounting board. While these mounts are fine for temporary or home use, they usually aren't acceptable for photographic contests or salons.

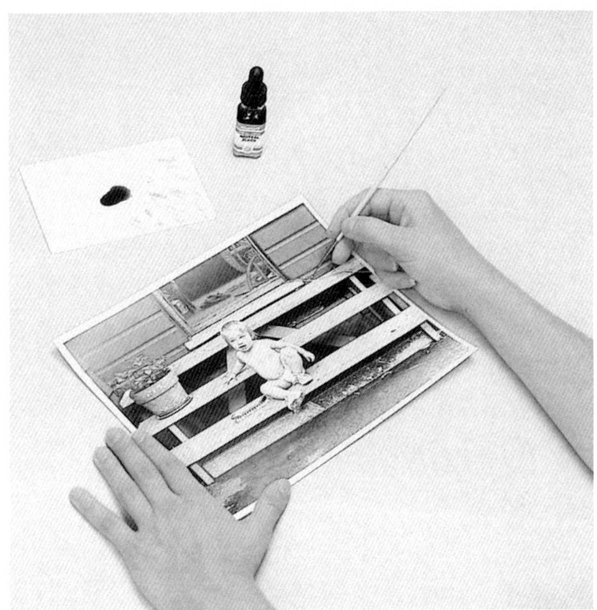

Apply the spotting color with a dotting or stippling motion until it matches the tone of the surrounding area—and the spot is no longer visible.

You may also mount your prints by using a photographically inert cement, such as KODAK Rapid Mounting Cement. This cement is packaged in small tubes and is especially suitable for mounting small prints in albums. Never use rubber cement for mounting paper-base prints; it may contain compounds that could stain your prints.

Spotting

Despite all the precautions you take against dust and dirt, most prints seem to end up with at lease a few white spots. You can fill in the spots by using a good-quality spotting brush with a fine point. For spotting black-and-white prints, you can use liquid spotting dyes available through photo dealers.

Using these spotting dyes lets you match any image tone by mixing only a few drops of dyes of different colors. For example, you can produce a wide range of sepia tones by mixing warm brown with black, and (if necessary) diluting the mixture with water.

Simply pick up the dye with your brush, wipe the excess dye off, and apply the dye to the white spot. Always check the amount of dye on the brush by stroking the brush on the margin of the print; then build up the dye gradually. Repeat until the spot matches the surrounding area.

Don't use a lot of dye on the brush! If you apply too much, reduce the spot by gently swabbing it with a brush and warm water that contains a few drops of dilute (non-detergent) ammonia. Blot with a tuft of dry cotton, and then dry the print before continuing.

CAUTION: Do not touch the brush to your lips or tongue to form a point. Even if the dyes are non-toxic, bacteria could be a problem.

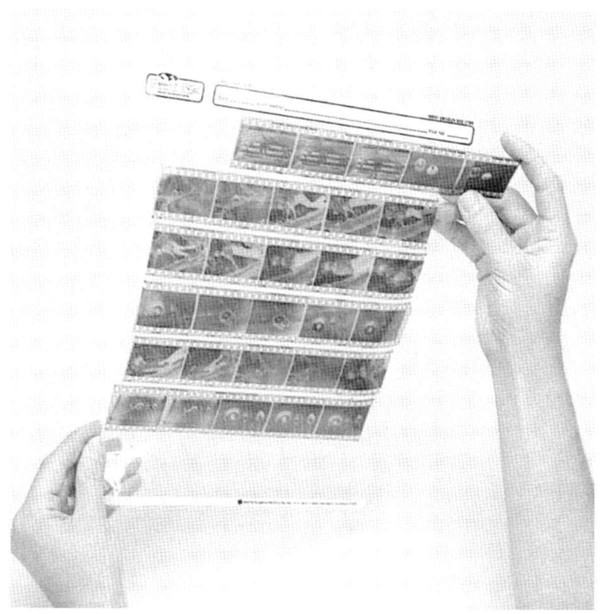

Your negatives will stay clean and unharmed when you file them properly.

Titling

Printing the title of your photograph and your name just below the print adds the finishing touch. Keep the title short and simple. Ideally, the first letter of the title should start even with the left edge of the print. Print your name in the lower right corner in letters to match the title. The last letter of your name should be flush with the right edge of the print.

Helpful Hints

Don't run off without filing your negatives safely for future use. For relocating a particular subject, it's a good idea to place an identifying number of the back of each print and on the negative sleeve or envelope.

Also, the cleaning chore will be much easier if you do it right away. Be sure to wash all the containers, trays, and thermometer. Discard the paper developer you used, even if you think you could squeeze through a few more prints. Developers don't keep well—even overnight—in open trays and in a partially exhausted condition.

Are there any fixer marks on the splashboard behind your sink or on the floor? Fixer-spotted darkrooms not only look messy; the fixer may become airborne. If fixer dust settles on photographic paper or film emulsion surfaces, it will cause small spots, called pinholes, on the emulsion.

The towels you used should be washed before your next printing session. This will help eliminate another possible source of mysterious spots on your negatives and prints. As you leave check to be sure that all the electric lights, including the safelight and the enlarger lamp, are turned off.

Darkrooms

How elaborate you make your darkroom will depend primarily on your needs, finances, and space. To develop an occasional roll of black-and-white film, almost any makeshift arrangement will do. If you want to make prints and enlargements, you may want a well-equipped room that is conveniently arranged and properly heated, lighted, and ventilated.

Darkroom Planning

The room must be lighttight. To check for stray light, stay in the darkroom for 5 minutes with all the lights turned off. After 5 minutes, if you can't see a sheet of white paper placed against a dark background, the room passes inspection. If there are light leaks, you will be able to see them because your eyes will have become adapted to the dark. Eliminate small light leaks with black tape. For large ones, such as the crack around a door, use dark heavy cloth or weather stripping. For your health and comfort, you should introduce a plentiful supply of clean, fresh air into your darkroom—especially during the chemical mixing and processing operations. Be sure to follow the safety recommendations on the product labels and in the instructions packaged with the processing chemicals. Check the photo magazines in your local library for articles on building lighttight darkroom ventilators.

Arrange your safelights so that they provide as much light as possible, but keep them at a safe distance—at least 4 feet (1.2 metres)—from your work area. Use a safelight equipped with a 15-watt bulb and the filter recommended on the paper (or film) instruction sheet. You can make a simple safelight test as follows:

1. Set your enlarging easel to give 1/2-inch white borders for the paper size you'll use in the test.
2. Place a normal-contrast negative typical of your work in the enlarger. Be sure the clear borders of the negative are completely masked.
3. Size and focus the image on the easel.
4. With all safelights on, make a good-quality print on grade 2 paper—or the paper you normally use. Process the paper normally (page 23) and dry it. Mark this print No. 1.
5. Turn the safelights off, and expose print No. 2 in the same way as print No. 1. Process and dry the paper, and mark it print No. 2.
6. With the safelights off, expose print No. 3 in the same way as print No. 2. Do not develop print No. 3.
7. With the safelights still off, place a piece of cardboard over the developing tray and put print No. 3 on it, emulsion side up. Safelight illumination is generally brightest in this location. Cover one-fourth of the print with an opaque card and turn on all the safelights. In the same way that you would make an exposure test strip, expose print No. 3 to the safelight for 1, 2, and 4 minutes, in steps. This gives four steps with safelight exposures of 0, 1, 3, and 7 minutes superimposed on the image exposure.
8. Develop this print for the same length of time as prints No. 1 and 2, with safelights turned off. Fix, wash, and dry the print in the normal manner.
9. Compare the prints. Prints No. 1 and 2 should be identical. If print No. 1 shows lower contrast or fogged highlights when compared with No. 2, you have a serious safelight problem. Be sure that the safelight filters (especially the one over the developing tray), bulb wattage, and distance and number of safelights are consistent with the recommendations on the paper instruction sheet.

If all three prints are identical, your safelight conditions are good. If print No. 3 shows slight fogging of highlights in any of the safelight-exposure areas, it is a warning to limit the exposure to safelight illumination to a time that will produce no fogging.

Note that fogging from safelight illumination will show up in areas that have already received some exposure before it will show up in the white borders. For this reason, safelight fog may go unnoticed unless the safelights are tested correctly.

In planning a darkroom, the main objective is to arrange your equipment and materials for efficiency and convenience. One of the most important requirements is to provide for a flow of work that can be done in the least amount of time with minimum effort. Another consideration is cost. Some other features and suggestions you should consider in setting up your darkroom are on the following pages.

For more information on building a darkroom, see Publication KW-14, *Building a Home Darkroom,* described on page 67.

CAUTION: Some photographic chemicals, particularly acid solutions, may cause corrosion. To minimize the chances of damage to your sink and drainage system, use cold water to wash the sink and flush the drain thoroughly after each use.

Temporary Darkroom

For developing black-and-white films and making prints, you can get started with only a minimum of equipment, plus an easily darkened kitchen, bathroom, closet, or any other room that has an electrical outlet. For night work, you can use practically any room as a darkroom; however, you should pull the shades or cover the windows with some dark material to exclude light from streetlamps, car headlights, or nearby lighted windows. It's convenient but not necessary to have a sink and a supply of water in the same room. The kitchen is probably the most convenient place to set up a temporary darkroom, since it is supplied with running water and electrical outlets, and the sink and counters provide adequate working space.

When space is not available for setting up a permanent darkroom and you must work in a room regularly used for other purposes, darkroom convenience sometimes has to be sacrificed. However, always try to arrange your equipment to allow a smooth, convenient flow of work from your enlarger through the developer and stop bath to fixing and washing. You should have a large tray filled with water for washing your prints. The KODAK Automatic Tray Siphon is a handy gadget for converting an ordinary tray into an efficient print washer. You should also have a container of water to rinse the solutions from your hands. This helps prevent contamination of your developer with other solutions. Use a clean towel to dry your hands thoroughly before handling film, negatives, and photographic paper. Group your equipment so that you can perform all operations with a minimum of steps, but allow sufficient working space. One suggested arrangement for a kitchen darkroom is shown in Figure 1.

It is helpful to have a table or other separate work area on which you can perform all the dry operations, such as printing and loading film tanks. This prevents water and solutions from splashing on equipment and dry materials. Set up all wet processing operations in or near the sink.

If there is no lamp socket over your processing area, use an extension cord to suspend the safelight over the processing trays. Keep the safelight at least 4 feet from your trays. A good safelight to use in this manner is the KODAK 2-Way Safelamp, available from photo dealers. This V-shaped

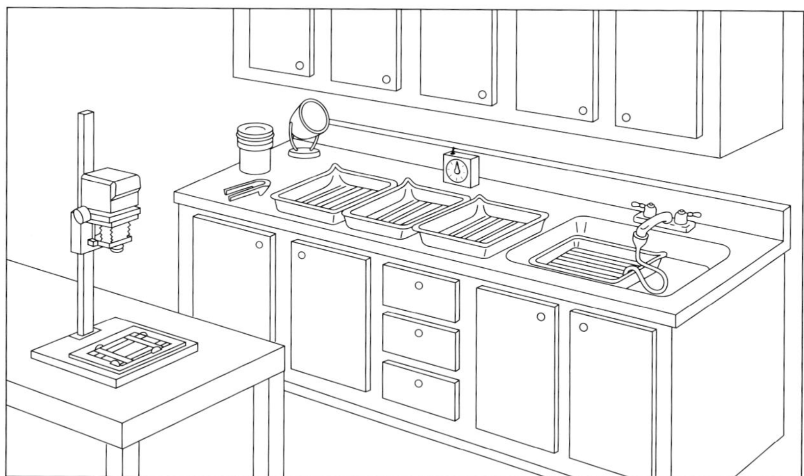

Figure 1 *Temporary Kitchen Darkroom*

safelight directs the light in two directions at once. You can screw it into the lamp socket of an extension cord or into a ceiling socket.

The best way to develop your film, especially in a temporary darkroom, is to use a film-developing tank, such as a Paterson Tank. Since these tanks are lighttight, any light that might leak into your darkroom would affect the film only during the time you are loading it into your tank. This minimizes the danger of light fogging your film, a frequent source of trouble. Check for stray light in your darkroom by following the procedure described on page 48 under "Darkroom Planning." After you have placed the cover on your film tank, you can turn on the white lights during development and the remainder of the processing steps.

With a temporary darkroom, it is important to consider ways of reducing the time and energy required to prepare the room for use and to clean it up afterwards. For instance, keeping all of your darkroom equipment in one or two boxes reduces both the time spent collecting equipment and the chance of misplacing something.

While the kitchen usually makes the best temporary darkroom, other rooms will serve. One possibility is a bathroom. However, although it has running water and electricity, there is usually no work surface to support trays and apparatus. You can make a work surface by placing a piece of plywood on the bathtub, but processing trays will be uncomfortably low. Sometimes it's possible to set up a card table to hold your trays and printing equipment. Protect the tabletop from spilled solutions by covering it with a piece of plastic such as a plastic tablecloth.

You can also use a small closet for a temporary darkroom. A closet is usually easy to make dark, even in the daytime. However, it will probably not have running water, and it may not have electrical outlets. If your closet has shelves, perhaps one of them is located at a convenient height If not, you may be able to install a removable shelf or bring in a small table. In any case, use plastic sheeting under the trays to catch any spilled solutions.

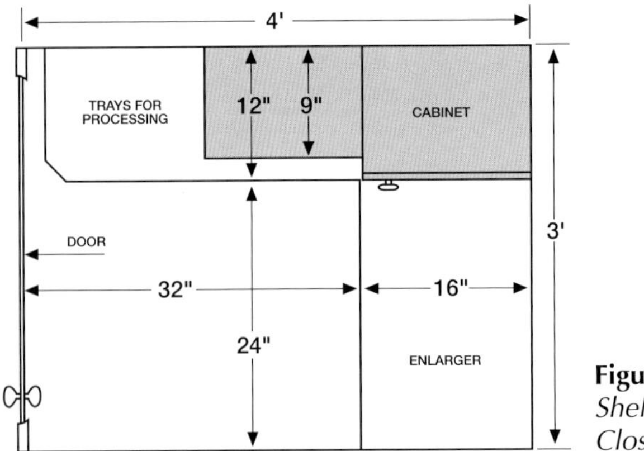

Figure 2
Shelves for a Closet Darkroom

Permanent Darkroom in a Small Closet

A permanent darkroom makes darkroom work much more convenient and saves a lot of setup time. If you have only a small closet available for use as a darkroom, make sure you utilize the space most efficiently.

A closet, of course, will not have running water, but this is not too important if there is a sink nearby where you can wash your negatives and prints. However, the closet must have electricity available. If there is no light socket in the closet, it is usually easy and inexpensive to have one or two outlets installed. It is best to have one socket in the ceiling for the white light and a double electrical outlet on the wall above the bench for plugging in your safelight and enlarger. Have a licensed electrician install or inspect the wiring to make sure that all wiring conforms to the electrical wiring code.

Figure 2 shows the arrangement of shelves for transforming a 3 x 4-foot closet into a darkroom suitable for developing film and making contact prints and enlargements up to 10 x 12 inches. The 12-inch shelf is 36 inches from the floor and holds the developing, stop bath, and fixing trays. The 16-inch shelf is the same height and supports your printer or enlarger.

A cabinet in the corner (upper right corner of drawing) on the wall above the processing shelf provides convenient and safe storage for your paper supply. A shelf about 9 inches wide, 2 feet above the processing shelf, extends along the wall next to the cabinet and provides shelf space for a timer and other small items. This shelf should extend no farther than approximately 15 inches from the end of the processing shelf so that it does not block the safelight illumination above your developing tray. Mount a safelight, such as a KODAK 2-Way Safelamp, on the wall or ceiling no closer than 4 feet from the processing shelf. You can store bottles of processing solutions on the floor under the tray shelf.

A Recommended Darkroom

Although you can produce good work in a closet darkroom, it is preferable to have a larger darkroom equipped with running water. With more room, you can make bigger prints, and you'll have space for additional equipment. For example, in the darkroom we are going to describe, you can conveniently process color film and make color prints.

Location

Where you decide to locate your darkroom will depend primarily on the space available. However, you should also consider convenience, temperature, and humidity.

Although a room on the first or second floor is suitable for a darkroom, a dry basement is usually the ideal location. If your basement is damp, you can make it dry by using a dehumidifier, available from appliance and department stores. The ideal relative humidity for darkroom work is about 50 percent; the ideal temperature is between 65 and 75°F (18 and 24°C). It is usually easier to maintain this temperature in a basement than in any other part of the house. Furthermore, hot-and cold-water connections and electrical connections are generally available in a basement. Another advantage is the ease of making a basement light-tight. Most basements have only a few small windows that you can easily cover with a piece of fiberboard or dark cloth. One more advantage of the basement darkroom is that spilled solutions are likely to cause little damage. However, all spilled solutions should be wiped up immediately.

A damp basement without a dehumidifier is not a good location for a permanent darkroom. Dampness causes mildew and rust on supplies and equipment. It also causes deterioration of films and papers, which results in weak, mottled pictures. However, if you must use a damp location, store your chemicals, films, and printing papers where it is cool and dry, and move them to your darkroom only when you need them.

An attic is another location that is usually not satisfactory for use as a darkroom. Unless it is well-insulated, an attic is likely to be too hot in the summer and too cold in the winter. Also, it is usually difficult and expensive to install plumbing in an attic.

Size

The darkroom shown in Figure 3 (on page 54) is designed to provide the utmost convenience in the flow of work. The space used for such a darkroom should preferably be neither smaller than 6 x 7 feet nor larger than 10 x 12 feet. The plan shown will fit within these limits.

You can close off the darkroom space from the rest of the area with partitions of wallboard. Partitions will prevent light from entering the darkroom if someone opens the door to the basement. As a precaution, put a sign that reads DARK—DO NOT ENTER on your darkroom door to show that the room is in use.

Capability

You can use the darkroom illustrated in Figure 3 for both black-and-white and color work. It is designed so that you can process roll film or sheet film, make proof sheets, and make enlargements up to 11 x 14 or 16 x 20 inches.

You can also readily adapt the room for other types of work, such as copying. The darkroom layout is arranged so that you can work efficiently with a minimum of wasted motion. It is also designed so that two or more people can divide the various operations and work together without interference. You can provide for drying negatives by stringing spring-type clothespins or film clips on a galvanized wire suspended between two walls. Use the clothespins or film clips to hold your negatives by the edges while they dry.

Arrangement

The darkroom work units shown in Figure 3 consist of a dry bench and a wet unit, each 26 inches wide and 6 feet long. You can either have them built in a woodworking shop or assemble them yourself from ready-made kitchen cabinets.

Use the dry bench for making prints and for handling film, negatives, and photographic paper. Since storage space for supplies and accessories is very important for work in this area, drawers and shelves are

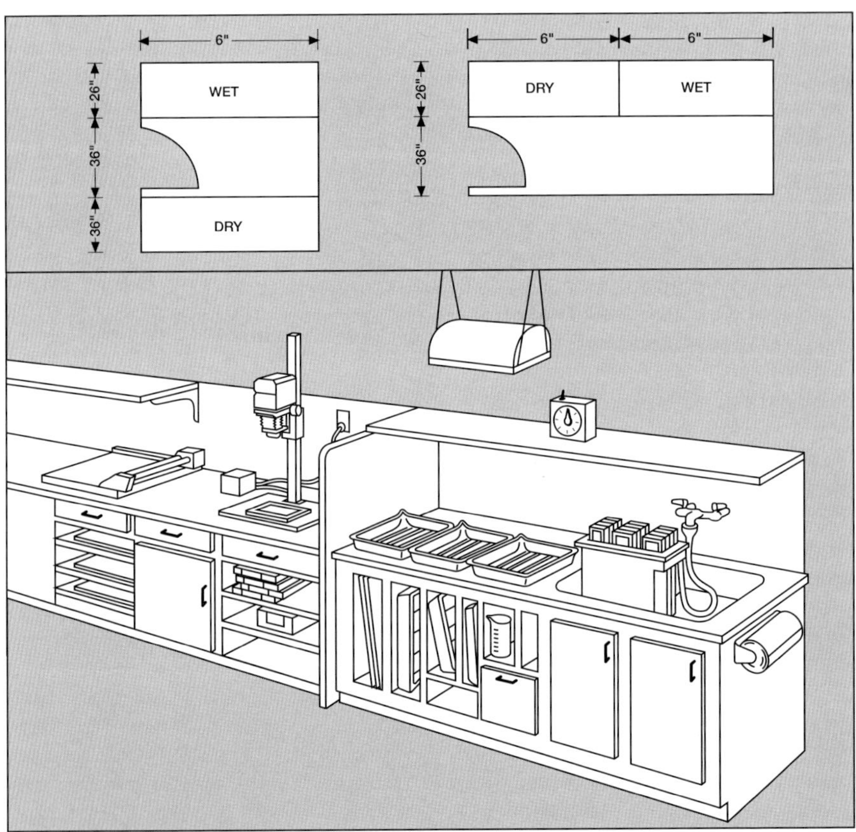

Figure 3 *Recommended Permanent Darkroom*

provided. Also, it is convenient to have a lighttight drawer, or dark drawer, near your equipment. This will provide quick access to photographic paper when you are making prints, and will eliminate the necessity of opening and closing the package of paper every time you need a sheet of paper. When you have finished printing, you should return the unused paper to its original package.

To make a dark drawer lighttight, install a sliding lid that fits in a groove around the top perimeter of the drawer. Paint the inside of the drawer and the lid flat black. Attach a small block of wood on the top of the lid and another one on the underside of the countertop. The blocks of wood will push the lid closed when you close the drawer.

You can use the space on top of the wet (or sink) unit for mixing chemicals and for all processing operations. Storage space for processing trays and chemical solutions is beneath this bench. Shelves mounted 2 feet above each unit provide storage space for bottles of stock solution, timers, thermometers, and other small equipment. Wooden pegs mounted on the splash guard provide a place to keep graduates. A towel holder mounted near the sink provides a towel for drying your hands.

You can locate the dry and wet units either on opposite sides of the darkroom with ample space between them or side by side with a splash guard separating them. With either arrangement, your equipment and materials will be protected from splashes from the wet work area.

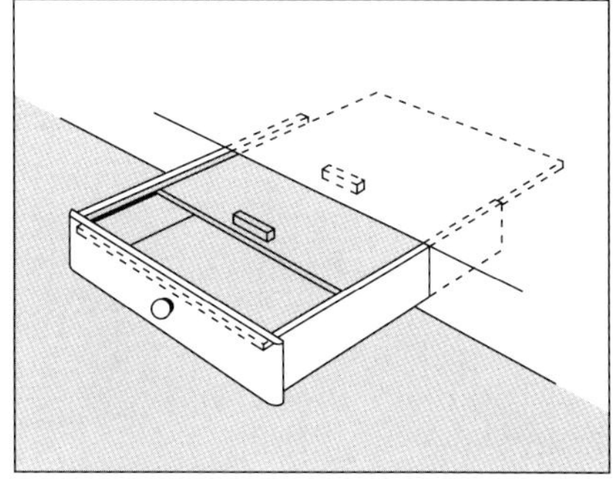

Figure 4 *Dark Drawer*

A safelight is suspended over each unit no closer than 4 feet from the working surface. To provide safelight illumination for the dry bench, you can use a safelight, such as a KODAK Darkroom Lamp or a KODAK 2-Way Safelamp, with the proper safelight filter. For the processing area, we recommend a larger safelight, such as the KODAK Utility Safelight Lamp, Model D. Double electrical outlets, properly grounded, are mounted over the units for plugging in your enlarger and other equipment.

A hot-and-cold mixing faucet is mounted over the sink. The nozzle should be at least 15 inches above the sink bottom to provide space for filling gallon bottles.

Because water and solutions will be spilled on the wet unit, it should have a waterproof surface. An excellent material for this is sheet plastic, commonly known as Formica®, widely used for kitchen counters and tabletops. Sheet plastic has an extremely hard surface that is resistant to most stains and corrosion. It is available in a variety of attractive colors and is easy to keep clean. You can purchase this material in sheets and cement it to the top of the unit, or you can purchase it as a laminate on plywood, a form that's easier to install. You can also obtain a professional custom-made plastic counter top; most cities have firms that specialize in such products.

If you don't install a waterproof covering, the joints in the bench top must be tight enough to prevent solutions from dripping onto the shelf below. Also, to protect the wood, coat the bench top with a chemical-resistant paint or lacquer.

Equipment Placement

If you study your work pattern in the darkroom, you can readily see the reasons for the recommended arrangement of the bench units and equipment. To make enlargements, for example, you take the package of photographic paper from the paper-storage shelf, open it, and place the paper in the dark drawer. After placing your negative in the enlarger and composing the image on the enlarging easel, you place a sheet of printing paper in the easel and expose it. (For proof sheets, you can place your printing frame on the bench next to the enlarger.) After the paper is exposed, you pass it on to the developer and the rest of the processing solutions. Then you wash your prints in the sink or in a tray equipped with a print washer.

When you have completed your work, you can place all equipment—including the easel and trimming board—on a shelf below the bench. This leaves the bench top clear for other activities.

One last point to remember: Darkroom cleanliness is very important for making pictures of high quality. Rinse the processing equipment you have used with water, and wipe the work surfaces clean with a damp viscose sponge.

Special Things to Do

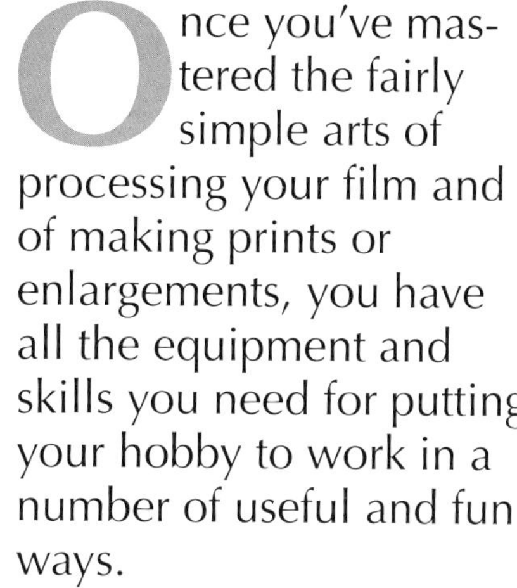

Once you've mastered the fairly simple arts of processing your film and of making prints or enlargements, you have all the equipment and skills you need for putting your hobby to work in a number of useful and fun ways.

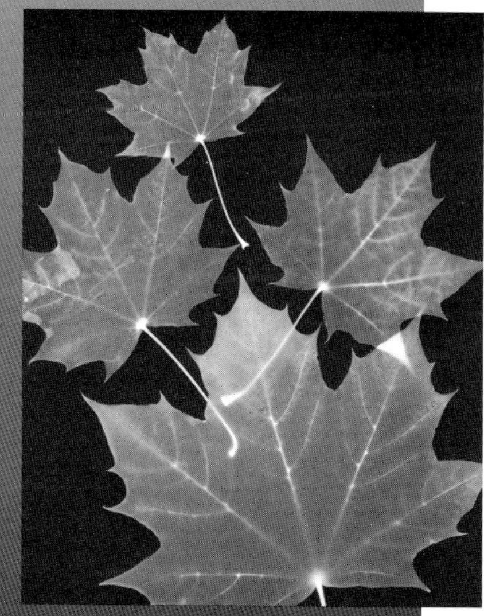

Photograms

A photogram is an illustration made on a sheet of photographic paper without using a negative. It consists of white or gray designs on a black background. The high-contrast appearance of a photogram is dramatic, and clever photograms are easy to make. All you need are a few small props and some photographic paper.

Under suitable safelight conditions, arrange some opaque or semi-opaque objects on a sheet of photographic paper with the emulsion side of the paper facing up. Leaves, shells, paper cutouts and letters, and even your hand or a pair of scissors are just a few good props for making photograms. When the arrangement suits you, turn on the exposing light. Use the light from your enlarger or a 7-watt light bulb. You'll probably need to experiment a bit with exposure time, depending on your light source. Process the paper in the usual way, and you'll have an original photographic creation!

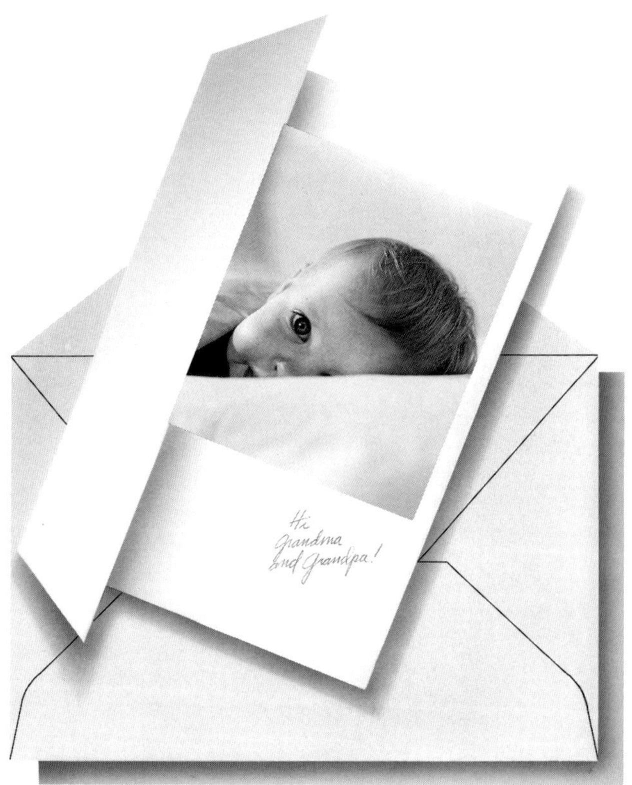

Greeting cards are fun to make and are uniquely personal. They let your creative urge run wild.

Greeting Cards

Maybe you've noticed that you seem to receive more and more photo-greeting cards each year. There's a good reason for the trend. Such cards are fun to make and are uniquely personal. They let your creative urge run wild.

There are lots of ways to make such cards. You can take a picture with a built-in greeting, such as someone writing on a blackboard. You can combine one of your negatives with another negative containing a suitable message. Or you might prefer slipping a print into a commercially made Christmas or other holiday folder. Your photo dealer will help you with ideas and materials. And although we've been talking about holiday cards, there's no reason why you shouldn't make your own photographic birth announcements or other special-events cards.

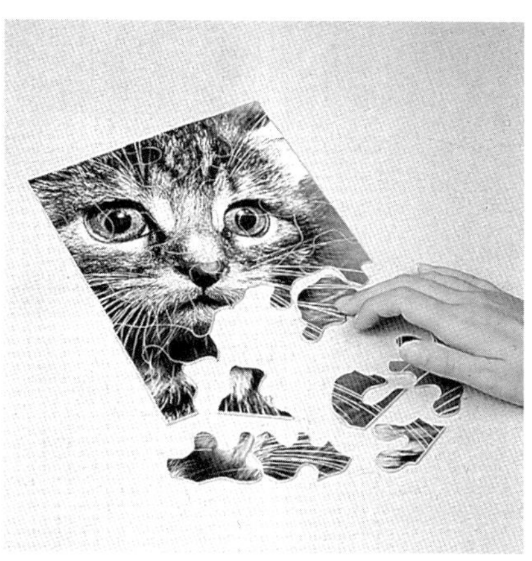

Photo Jigsaw Puzzles

Making a photo jigsaw puzzle is simple and a lot of fun. All that's needed are a mounted print (with a border of at least 1 inch), a pattern, photographic mounting cement, a straightedge, and a utility knife and blades.

To make a pattern, begin with a piece of paper the same size as the mount your print is on. Make an outline the size of your print. Draw the pieces along the border first, slowly working toward the middle until the pattern is complete. Remember that the pieces must interlock to form the puzzle effect.

Next cement the pattern to the borders of your print. Be sure to align it carefully. With the utility knife, start cutting in the middle of the picture, leaving the cuts around the border till last. Always use caution when working with sharp instruments. To protect your working surface, place an extra piece of mounting board or other suitable material under the print.

When all the cutting between the pieces has been done, trim the borders. To avoid a light border on the finished puzzle, use a straightedge as a guide to trim the puzzle slightly smaller than the original print. Your puzzle is now complete!

It's a good idea to store your puzzle in a box. If you're giving it as a gift, why not make a copy of the original print and paste it onto the box as identification?

Photo Essays

This isn't strictly darkroom advice—but it's so important we think it's worth a word. One of the important things some people do with pictures is to make reports, whether they're for work, or a club project, or a school requirement. When you step into the darkroom to make such pictures, here are some things to keep in mind.

The pictures should show very little except what's necessary to make the point. Crop your prints to show only the things that are important. Use captions to direct attention to what isn't obvious. Make the prints match in size and be relatively uniform in tone.

If you're making prints to mount in an album, 31/2-inch-square prints are about as small as you should make. If the prints are to be on a bulletin board or easel, 8 x 8 inches is the smallest size usually appropriate. In most display areas, lighter prints are easier to see than darker prints. Good picture sequences are planned ahead of time, not made in the darkroom.

Paper and Chemicals

Kodak offers a large variety of black-and-white photographic papers, each with different characteristics, from which you can select the paper that will produce the best possible prints from your negatives.

Choosing a Paper

The characteristics of photographic papers are divided into two general classes—photographic and physical. The photographic characteristics of a paper describe its contrast grade and its speed. The physical characteristics describe its coating, image tone, surface, base tint, and weight.

Photographic Characteristics

Contrast Grade

Kodak makes papers of several contrast grades so that you can make good prints from negatives of different contrasts. Some negatives have low contrast—little difference in blackness (density) between their light and dark areas. Other negatives have normal contrast. Still others have high contrast. To produce normal contrast in your prints, use low-contrast paper with high-contrast negatives, and high-contrast paper with low-contrast negatives. Use contrast grade:

No. 1 *for negatives with high contrast.*

No. 2 *for negatives with normal contrast.*

No. 3 *for negatives with somewhat less contrast than normal.*

No. 4 *for negatives with low contrast.*

Some Kodak papers are available in five contrast grades, ranging from No. 1 for printing very-high-contrast negatives to No. 5 for printing very-low-contrast negatives. Other papers are supplied in only one contrast grade for use with normal-contrast negatives. Papers such as KODAK POLYCONTRAST III RC Paper have variable contrast; you can change the contrast of the paper by using filters.

Speed

Paper speed indicates the paper sensitivity to light and is much less than that of most films. Enlarging papers are higher in speed than contact papers, but you can use most Kodak enlarging papers for contact printing as well if you reduce illumination in the contact printer. Contact papers require a high-intensity light source, and most enlarging lamps lack the illumination required for using contact papers.

Physical Characteristics

Resin Coating

Resin-coated (RC) papers have a water-resistant base to help prevent penetration by processing chemicals. This reduces the time needed for processing, washing, and drying the paper. It also eliminates the need for ferrotyping. Use an F-surface RC paper if you want glossy prints. This surface has a built-in gloss.

Image Tone

Image tone is the color of the photographic image in the finished print. When the image of the print tends toward brown, it's called warm in tone; when the image tends toward blue; it's called cold in tone. Image-tone designations for Kodak papers are blue-black, neutral-black, warm-black, and brown-black. When you plan to use a chemical toner, select a

BEST BET

Use POLYCONTRAST III RC Paper or POLYMAX RC Paper to start. As you advance in your printing skills, there are other papers to meet all types of display needs, such as ELITE Fine-Art Paper for making fine display prints.

paper with an image tone that is compatible with the toner. See the instructions that come with the paper or toner. For information on toning, see KODAK Publication G-23, *Toning KODAK Black and White Materials*, available from Kodak, Dept. 412-L, Rochester, NY 14650.

Surface

Surface sheen is the characteristic of papers that describes the degree of shininess of the paper surface. The glossier the surface, the blacker the apparent maximum density and the greater the possible range of tones in the print. Kodak papers come in the following sheens:

Glossy paper is a good choice when you want the most brilliant prints and the best reproduction of fine detail, such as for album prints and for pictures to be published in books and magazines.

High Lustre paper has a sheen slightly less than that of glossy paper and almost as great a black-to-white range. It's especially suitable for producing prints that require a great deal of brilliance without ferrotyping.

Lustre and Semi-Matt papers have a lower sheen than glossy or high lustre papers. Smooth semi-matt surfaces (A and N) accept retouching readily. E and G lustre surfaces are used widely for display prints such as portraits.

Base Tint

Base tint is the color of your paper stock. Your choice of tint will depend on your subject and the kind of paper you want to use. Kodak papers are furnished in the following tints:

White is recommended for cold-toned subjects—snow scenes, seascapes—and for high-key pictures and prints you want to tone blue. It's also good for general use.

Cream White is also an excellent choice for general subjects. It's well-suited to subjects photographed in either daylight or artificial light.

Weight

Weight describes the thickness of the paper stock. Kodak papers come in Single Weight (SW), Medium Weight (MW), and Double Weight (DW). Double-weight and medium-weight papers are preferable for enlargements because of better handling characteristics.

CONTACT PAPER

KODAK AZO Paper is an excellent choice for making contact prints from negatives of general subjects. Do not use contact paper with an enlarger. Use a printing frame and a 7-watt light bulb. See page 22, step 7.

ENLARGING PAPERS

KODABROMIDE Paper is a fast general-purpose enlarging paper. It has high speed and exceptional development latitude: contrast and image tone remain uniform over a wide range of exposure and development times. This makes KODABROMIDE Paper a good choice for fast production of prints from a wide variety of negatives.

KODABROME II RC Paper is a medium-weight high-speed enlarging paper with a warm-black tone on a water-resistant base for general use. The F surface requires no ferrotyping. It is available in contrast grades numbered 1 through 5.

KODAK POLYCONTRAST III RC Paper is a high-speed variable-contrast enlarging paper of warm-black tone on a medium-weight, resin-coated base. Optical brighteners provide great visual impact through whiter whites and a longer apparent tonal range. A water-resistant base shortens fixing, washing, and drying times and eliminates the need for ferrotyping with the F-surface paper.

You can produce any of several contrast grades from the same package of paper when you expose your print through filters, such as KODAK POLYMAX Filters. By using these filters, you can vary the contrast of the papers in 12 half-grade steps from Grade -1 through Grade 5+. No filter is required with normal-contrast negatives and tungsten-light enlargers. Selective dodging is possible when you expose one part of your print through one filter and the rest through another filter to achieve the desired contrast throughout.

KODAK EKTALURE Paper is excellent for exhibit prints and portraits. It's a fast enlarging paper that has a warm, brown-black image tone. The speed of EKTALURE Paper makes it a good choice for fast production of high-quality prints. This paper tones easily in such toners as KODAK POLY-TONER and KODAK Rapid Selenium Toner.

KODAK PANALURE SELECT RC Paper is a high-speed enlarging paper designed for making black-and-white prints from color negatives. PANALURE SELECT RC Paper contains an optical brightener that adds brilliance to the prints. The water-resistant, resin-coated base of this paper allows rapid processing and drying, and eliminates the need for ferrotyping.

KODAK POLYFIBER Paper is a general-purpose selective-contrast enlarging paper with a neutral-black tone and optical brighteners. It is available in double, single, and light weights. You can produce any of 12 different contrasts in half-grade increments from Grade -1 to Grade 5+ from the same package of paper when you expose your prints through KODAK POLYMAX Filters. You can expose one part of your print through one filter and the rest through another to achieve the contrasts you need for different areas of a print.

KODAK ELITE Fine-Art Paper is an excellent choice for making superior display prints. Its neutral-black tone and optical brighteners provide whiter whites and a longer apparent tonal range when you view the prints under fluorescent lights or in daylight. This gives a tonal range from brilliant white highlights to deep rich blacks. The extremely high-quality extra-thick paper base of densely packed fibers makes this paper especially resistant to damage in handling. This is very important when you make large prints. ELITE Paper is available in four contrast grades. You can ferrotype or air-dry this paper.

KODAK POLYMAX RC Paper is a medium-speed selective-contrast enlarging paper. This medium-weight paper has a neutral-black tone and optical brighteners, and its water-resistant base means rapid processing and drying times. By exposing the paper through POLYMAX Filters, you can match the paper to negatives of different contrasts. Because there are no developing agents incorporated in the emulsion, development is slow enough that you also have control over the contrast during tray processing.

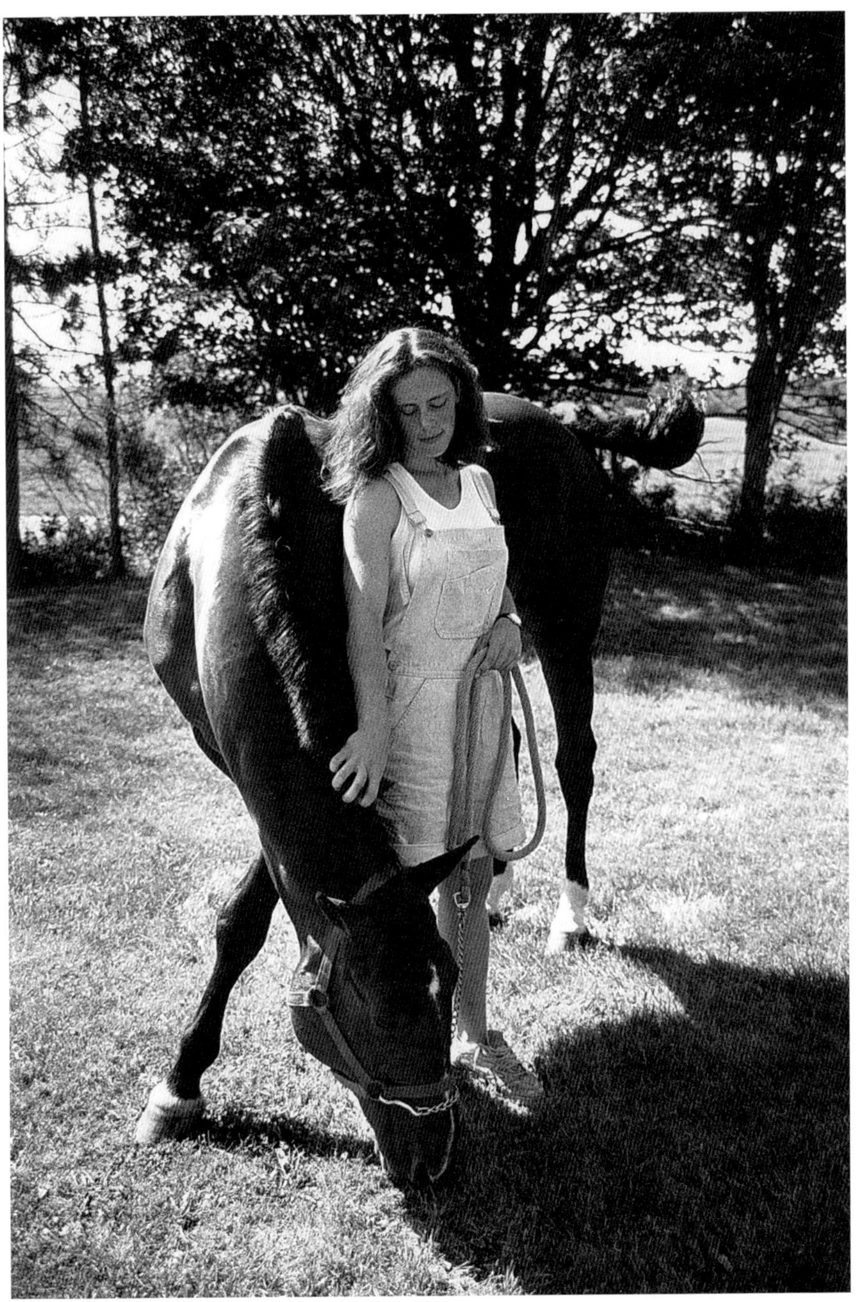

Enlargement made on KODAK POLYCONTRAST III RC Paper.

Chemicals

Kodak offers a variety of chemicals for black-and-white film and paper processing. Kodak chemicals come in units of different sizes to fill the needs of both the occasional printer and the printer who spends several evenings a week in the darkroom. If you do a lot of processing and printing, you'll probably want to buy the more economical, larger-size units.

Developers for Film

KODAK T-MAX Developer—A new liquid-concentrate film developer that offers improved shadow detail and higher image quality. Available in sizes to make 1 and 5 gallons of solution. Excellent for small-tank and rotary-tube processing of T-MAX, PLUS-X, and TRI-X Films.

KODAK Developer D-76—Offers full emulsion speed and greater shadow detail with normal contrast. Packed as a powder.

KODAK MICRODOL-X Developer—Offers maximum enlargeability. Packed as a powder.

KODAK HC-110 Developer—A highly active developer supplied in liquid-concentrate form for handy use. It produces negatives similar to those developed in Developer D-76 but with shorter development times.

Developers for Paper

KODAK DEKTOL Developer—For neutral and cold-tone images on cold-tone papers. High capacity, uniform development rate, good keeping.

KODAK SELECTOL-SOFT Developer—For producing less contrast with warm-tone papers.

KODAK POLYMAX T Developer—A liquid developer-concentrate for use with cold-tone papers.

KODAK EKTAFLO Developer, Type 2—A concentrated liquid developer for use with warm-tone papers.

Stop Bath

KODAK Indicator Stop Bath—Supplied in a concentrated liquid form. The solution is light yellow when mixed, appearing colorless under a safelight. It becomes purple when exhausted, appearing dark under a safelight.

Fixing Baths

KODAK POLYMAX T Fixer—A single-solution hardening fixer for papers. Designed for use with KODAK POLYMAX T Developer.

KODAK Fixer—A hardening fixing bath for all-purpose use with films, plates, and papers.

KODAFIX Solution—A general-purpose concentrated liquid hardening-fixing bath. It has long life and high capacity.

Processing Aids

KODAK Hypo Clearing Agent—Promotes faster and more thorough print washing.

KODAK PHOTO-FLO Solution—Minimizes watermarks and drying streaks on films, and speeds drying. You can start with the 4-ounce size—a little goes a long way.

Kodak Photo Books and Guides

The following KODAK Photo Books and guides will provide you with many inspirational ideas for new and different techniques, and present a wealth of reference material to help you in your darkroom. These and other KODAK Photo Books on a variety of photographic topics are available through your photo dealer.

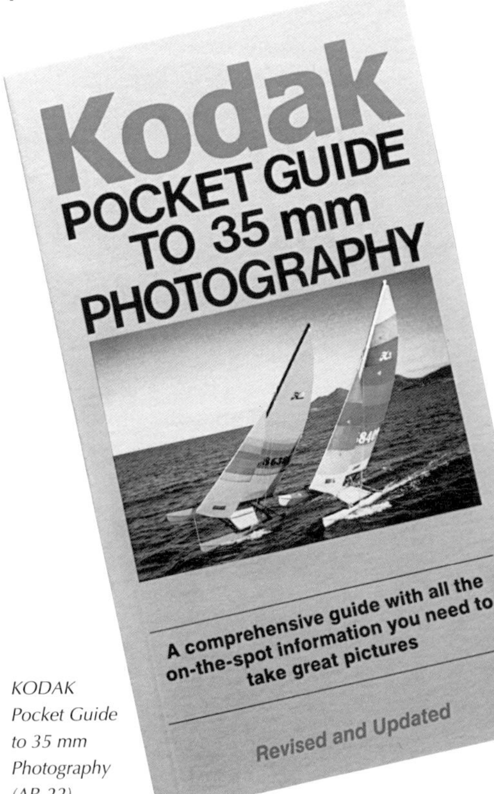

KODAK Pocket Guide to 35 mm Photography (AR-22)

DARKROOM BOOKS

Black-and-White Darkroom Techniques (KW-15)
Details steps for developing, printing, and finishing black-and-white photos, and describes a number of special processing and printing techniques. The book includes sections on choosing photographic paper, dodging and burning, mounting prints, and more.

8 1/2 x 11 inches, 96 pages

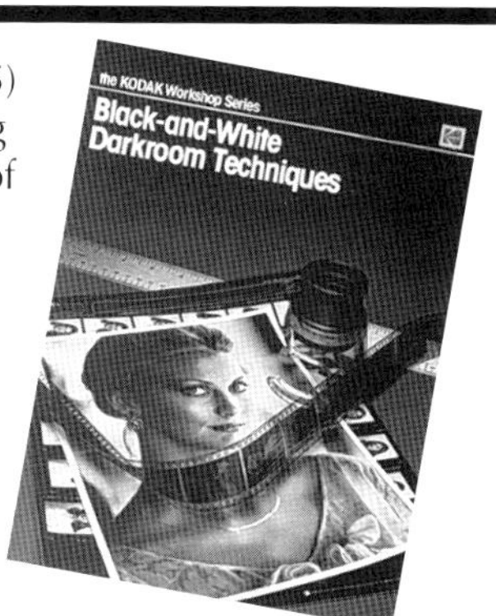

Building a Home Darkroom (KW-14)
Complete coverage of the steps and equipment needed for building an advanced home darkroom. Treatments include electricity, plumbing, construction materials, and safety. Possible locations and special situations are discussed, and the construction of a darkroom erected in the basement of an older home is outlined step by step.

8 1/2 x 11 inches, 96 pages

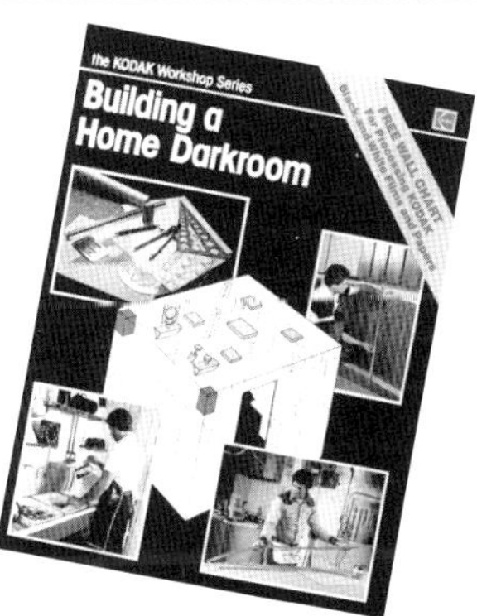

KODAK Black-and-White Darkroom DATAGUIDE (R-20)
Provides information on exposing film, controlling development, printing and processing for print stability, and toning. Also includes information and many applications on KODAK T-MAX Professional Films and T-MAX Developers.

5 7/8 x 8 3/4 inches, 66 pages

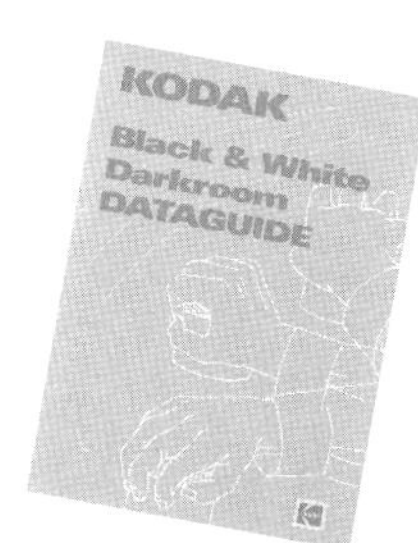

PHOTOGRAPHY BOOKS

Advanced Black-and-White Photography (KW-19)
Features techniques for achieving high quality at both camera and darkroom stages of making a photograph, with emphasis throughout on image control, appearance, and fine-art presentation. Also included is a section on hand coloring with step-by-step tips.

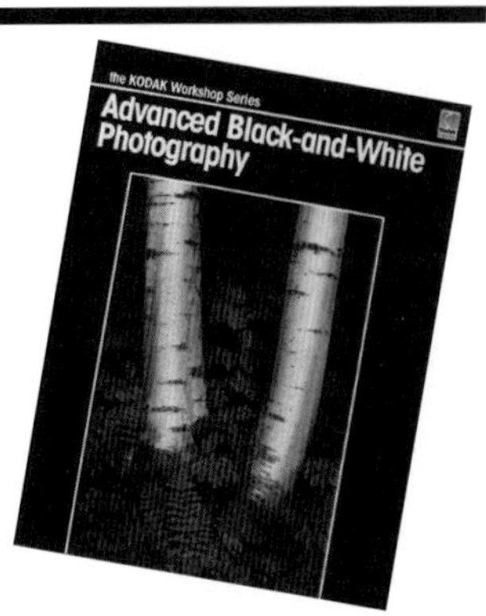

8 1/2 x 11 inches, 104 pages

KODAK Pocket Photoguide (AR-21)
Pocket-sized reference book on exposure, filters, films, flash, lenses, and other photographic essentials. The guide contains dial calculators, tables, and instructions for taking still pictures in color and black and white.

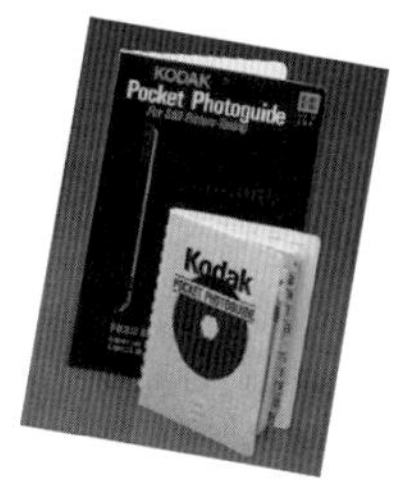

3 3/4 x 5 inches, 42 pages

Basic Developing, Printing, Enlarging in Color (AE-13)
Step-by-step information on processing color negative and color slide films and making color prints from negatives and slides. It's the companion to this book, **Basic Developing & Printing in Black and White** (AJ-2).

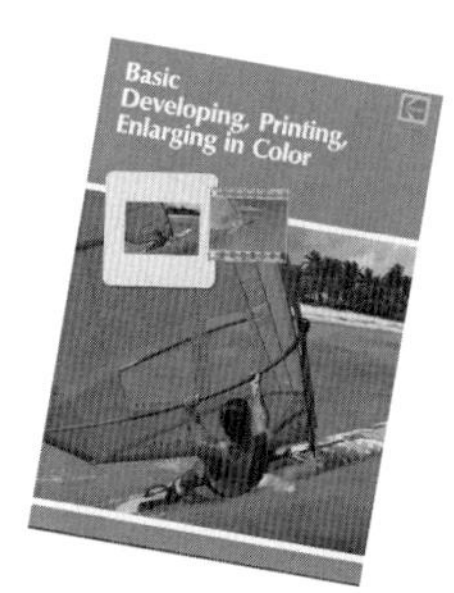

6 1/2 x 9 inches, 100 pages

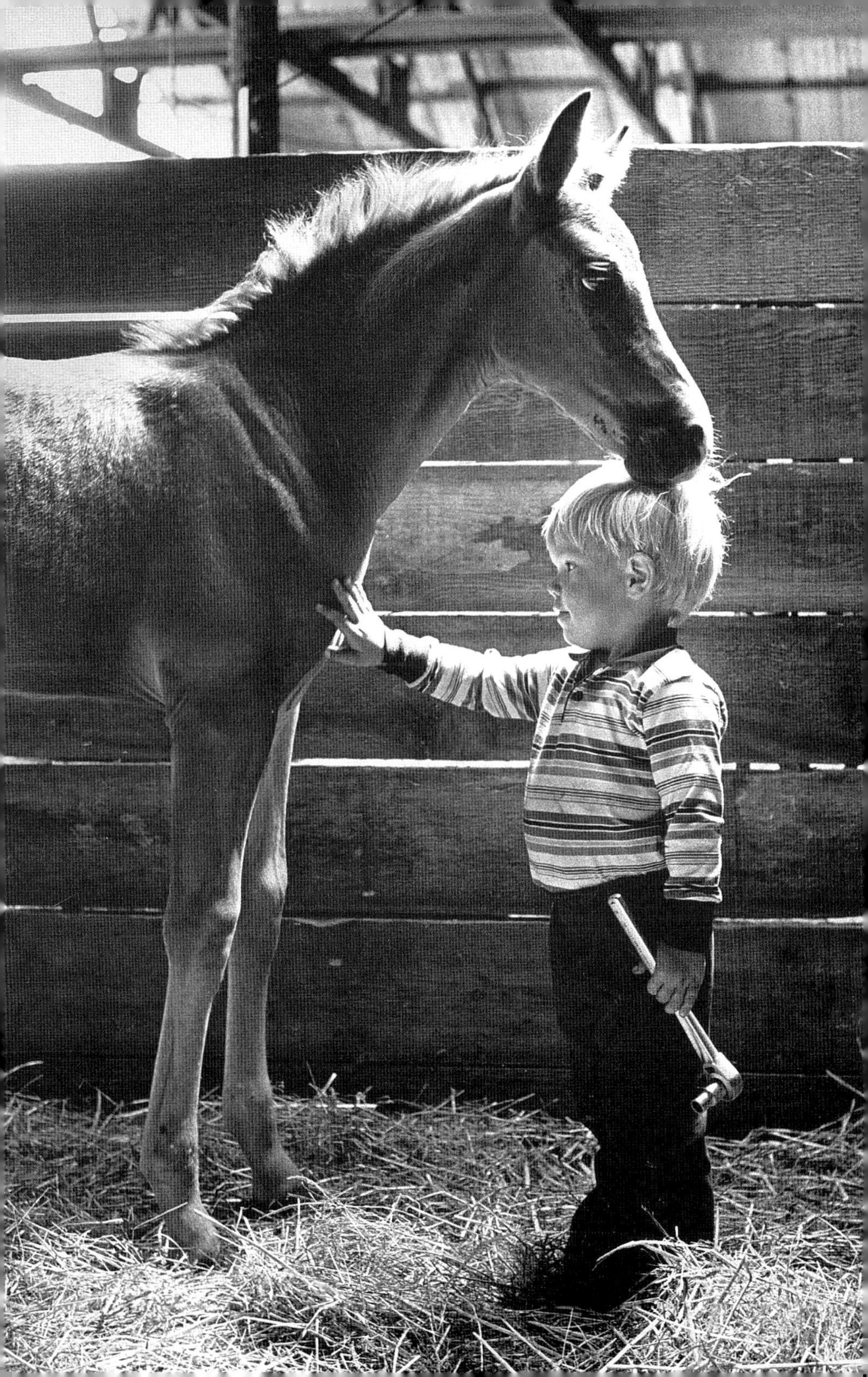

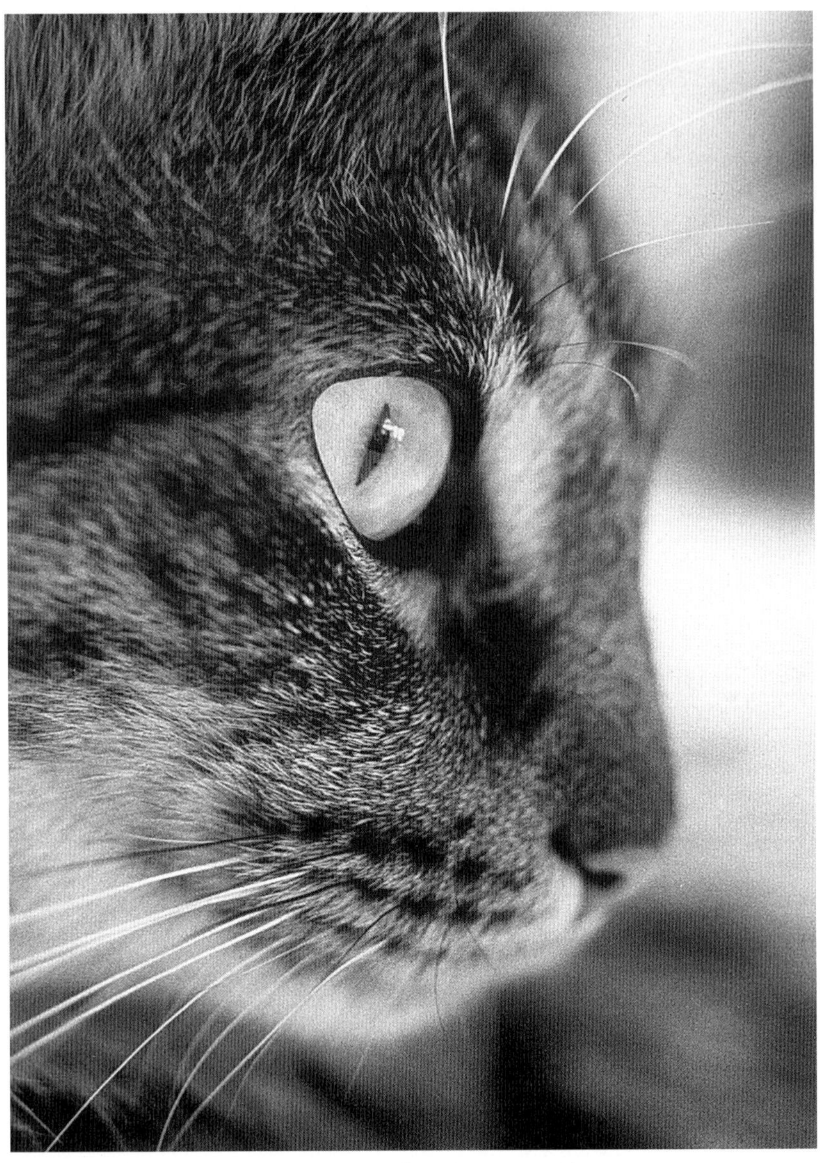

Cropping added even more impact to this close-up made on KODAK T-MAX 400 Professional Film.

Basic Equipment Checklist

Processing Film

1. Processing tank
2. Thermometer
3. Graduate
4. Film clips
5. 3 bottles
6. Timer
7. Developer, fixer, and stop bath
8. Stirring rod
9. Film squeegee

Printing

1. Printing frame or enlarger
2. 4 trays
3. Stirring rod
4. Graduate
5. 3 bottles
6. Safelight
7. Developer, fixer, and stop bath
8. Photographic paper
9. Thermometer
10. Timer
11. Print squeegee
12. Print tongs or rubber gloves

Print Processing Summary

At 68°F (20°C)

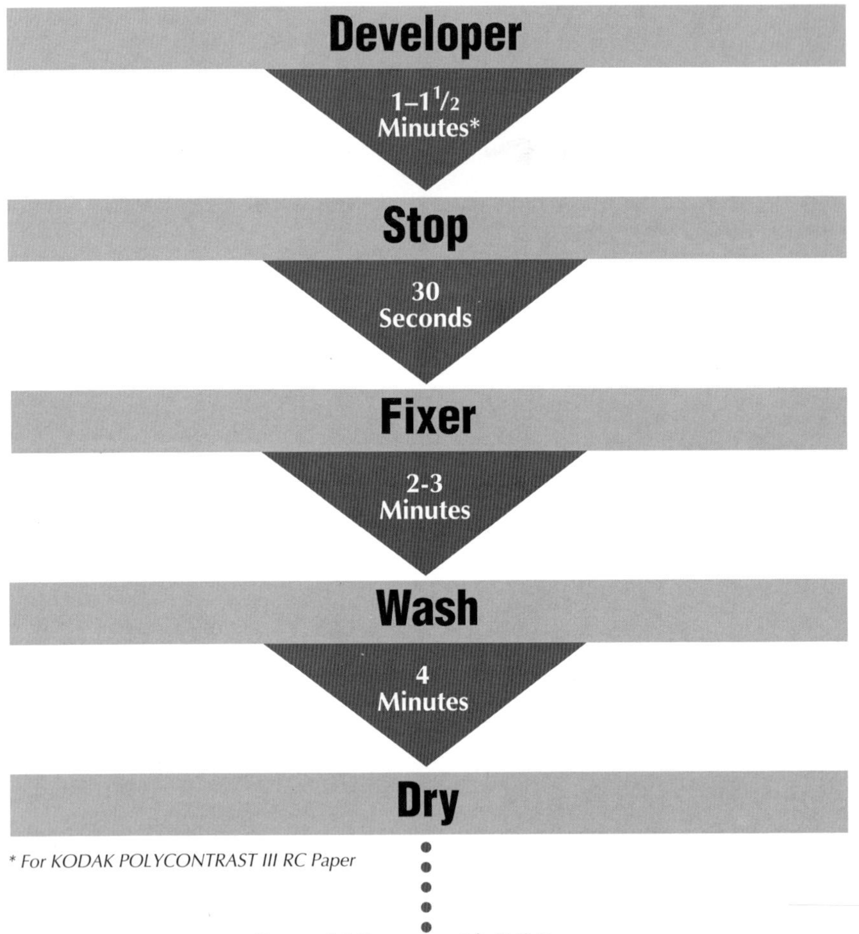

** For KODAK POLYCONTRAST III RC Paper*

Several Minutes with RC Paper

TIP

Save wash water by using KODAK Hypo Clearing Agent. See instructions on packaging.

For negatives, a similar summary could apply; the significant difference would be the development time for the particular film.